Fitting Finesse

Nancy Zieman

Fitting Finesse

©1994 by Oxmoor House, Inc.
Book Division of Southern Progress Corporation
P.O. Box 2463, Birmingham, Alabama 35201
Published by Oxmoor House, Inc., and Leisure Arts, Inc.

Library of Congress Number: 94-69580
Hardcover ISBN: 0-8487-1486-5
Softcover ISBN: 0-8487-1437-7
Manufactured in the United States of America
First Printing 1995

Editor-in-Chief: Nancy J. Fitzpatrick
Senior Homes Editor: Mary Kay Culpepper
Senior Crafts Editor: Susan Ramey Cleveland
Senior Editor, Editorial Services: Olivia Kindig Wells
Art Director: James Boone

Fitting Finesse

Editor: Lois Martin
Editorial Assistant: Laura A. Fredericks
Copy Editor: L. Amanda Owens
Copy Assistant: Jennifer K. Mathews
Designer: Emily Albright
Production and Distribution Director: Phillip Lee
Production Manager: Gail Morris
Associate Production Manager: Theresa L. Beste
Production Assistant: Marianne Jordan
Illustrators: Rochelle Stibb, Carol Loria, Kelly Davis
Editorial Assistance, Nancy's Notions: Susan Roemer
Photographers: Dale Hall, Keith Glasgow

Fitting Finesse is my painless approach to fitting—both for you and your pattern! Using my method, you'll be pleased to find that your valuable sewing time will always result in a garment with a comfortable, attractive fit.

Few of us have a runway model's shape, so chances are that your patterns need some fine-tuning. Fitting a garment may not seem like as much fun as choosing luscious fabrics or watching once flat yardage take dimensional shape, yet it's the most important part of sewing.

Many of us who learned to sew in junior high school probably cut patterns in sections and then taped them back together to add or subtract inches. If your results, or even the process, do not meet your expectations, it's time for a change. The Fitting Finesse approach is easy—no cutting, slashing, tucking, or pinching—just logical and easy pivot-and-slide techniques.

Why spend unnecessary hours fitting when you could be sewing? Read through the first chapter and then zero in on the areas where you need Fitting Finesse. It's that simple.

Happy fitting!

Nancy Zieman

Table of Contents

Blouse, Dress, and Jacket Fitting Finesse

Shortcuts and Specialized Fitting

Fitting Skirts with Finesse

Pants Fitting Finesse

Fine-tuning the Fit

Reference

Fitting Facts

People today look for fast, high-quality results, whether we're sending packages, eating in restaurants, visiting doctors, or sewing clothes—especially sewing clothes to *fit*.

Fitting is as integral to sewing as winding bobbins. Without the correct fit, our sewing projects just hang in the closet unworn.

A key to getting the right fit is carefully comparing eight specific body measurements with measurements from the pattern. Once you learn the pivot-and-slide techniques of fitting from this book, I'm sure you'll find it easy to make every garment you sew fit your size and shape.

Choosing the Right Pattern Size

The first stop en route to Fitting Finesse is finding your correct pattern size. You can't dial an 800 number for the right size but finding it is as simple as taking one measurement.

Those of you who have been sewing for several years will recognize that the common measurement used to choose size for a blouse, jacket, or top pattern is your bust measurement. This measurement is accurate if your figure is well proportioned, but if your bust is large in proportion to the rest of your body or if you have a broad back, the bust measurement gives you a pattern that fits your bust but gaps at the neckline, the shoulders, and the armholes. "Gaposis," as I call it, is a common fitting problem that is difficult to correct (Diagram A). The solution? Buy your pattern to fit your shoulder area.

The measurement I recommend using to determine which pattern size fits your shoulders is the front width measurement. You won't find the front width measurement printed on the back of the pattern envelope, but it's quick to take and does not change even if you gain or lose weight.

Note from Nancy: I find the front width measurement and other body measurements a challenge to take by myself, so I use the buddy system: I call a sewing buddy to help me, and I help her. This is the best way to assure accuracy. Be sure to take the front width measurement while you are wearing a slip or other undergarment so that your arm creases are evident.

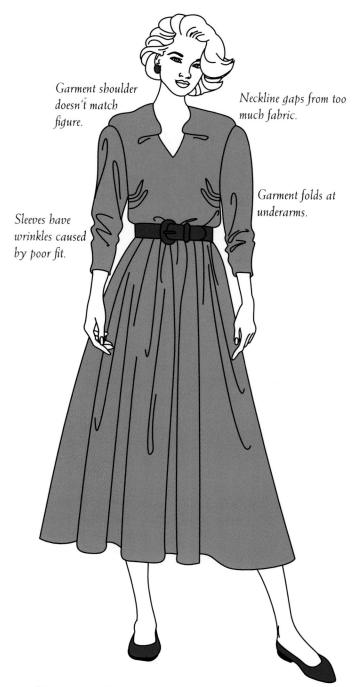

Garment shoulder doesn't match figure.

Neckline gaps from too much fabric.

Sleeves have wrinkles caused by poor fit.

Garment folds at underarms.

Diagram A: Choosing pattern size based on bust measurement can result in "gaposis."

Front Width Measurement

• Find the crease in your skin where your arm meets your body.

• Measure above the end of one crease straight across the front of your chest to the end of the other crease (*Diagram B*).

• Round off the measurement to the nearest ½".

Even though the front width measurement and its corresponding sizes are not written on the back of the pattern envelope, the sizing is easy to remember. Misses' size 14 equals 14", and the sizes go up or down with every ½". For example, if your measurement is 13½", buy a size 12. If you measure 14½", select a size 16.

Note from Nancy: If you are unsure which of two sizes to use, go with the smaller size. Remember, it is easier to fit the bust (to make it larger) than to fit the shoulder and neck area.

You may be pleasantly surprised by the results of the front width measurement. It is very common for someone who has been sewing with a size 20 in order to fit her bust to find out she is actually a size 16.

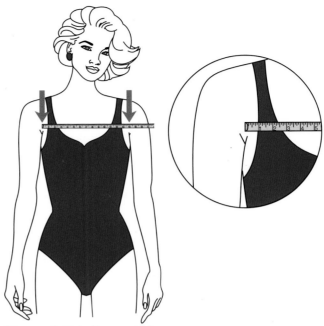

Diagram B: Take front width measurement above arm creases.

Fashion Fact: 60% of U.S. homes have sewing machines. — *The Sewing Fashion Council*

Front Width Fitting Chart												
Front width	12"	12½"	13"	13½"	14"	14½"	15"	15½"	16"	16½"	17"	17½"
Misses and Petites	6	8	10	12	14	16	18	20	22			
Juniors	5	7	9	11	13	15						
Half Size			10½	12½	14½	16½	18½	20½	22½	24½		
Women's							38	40	42	44	46	48

Taking Accurate Measurements

For most of your fitting, you'll need to take five width measurements and two length measurements, in addition to the front width measurement. (Pant measurements are slightly different; see page 91, "Measuring Your Figure," for details.) If you are buying a smaller size than you have in the past or if you are new to sewing, take all seven measurements. If your pattern size has not changed, consider measuring only the areas that you know are too tight, too loose, too long, or too short.

Earlier I recommended taking the front width measurement with the buddy system; use the same team approach for these measurements.

Note from Nancy: When taking measurements, don't worry about fractions less than ½". Our measurements fluctuate. (Just remember what an extra piece of chocolate cake can do to the fit of your waistband.) Always measure to the closest ½" and don't get hung up on differences of ¼" or less!

At the end of this book is a Personal Fitting Chart on page 141. Using the guidelines below, record your measurements on the chart as you and your sewing buddy measure your figure. Keep this book in your sewing room for quick reference. (Feel free to photocopy the fitting chart to use when fitting garments for friends and family.)

Bust

Measure around the fullest part of the bust, keeping the tape measure parallel to the floor. Measure to the closest ½".

When taking width measurements, place a thumb or a finger underneath the tape measure to prevent the

Diagram A: Place thumb or finger beneath tape measure when taking bust measurement.

Diagram B: When you bend to side, deepest wrinkle is your waist.

Diagram C: Measure to closest ½".

measurement from being taken too tightly (*Diagram A*).

Waist

Bend to the side; the deepest resulting wrinkle is your waist (*Diagram B*). Stand straight again and

measure around your waist, keeping the tape measure parallel to the floor. Place a thumb or a finger under the tape measure to prevent the measurement from being taken too tightly. Measure to the closest ½" (*Diagram C*).

Hip

Measure the fullest part of the hip, keeping the tape measure parallel to the floor and a finger underneath the tape to make sure it is not too tight. Measure to the closest ½" (Diagram D).

Take a second measurement—the hip length—measuring the distance between the waist and the hip. This measurement will let you mark hip placement, allowing you to add or to subtract from the pattern at your actual hip (Diagram E).

Note from Nancy: At the same time that I measure the width around my hip, I simply pick up the loose end of the tape measure to find the distance between my waist and hip.

Back Waist Length

Measure from the base of your neck to your waist. Find the base of your neck by bending your head forward until the prominent bone at the base of the neck is easily felt. Straighten your neck and measure from that bone down your back to the waist (Diagram F).

Back Width

Measure from one side to the other across the back, directly above the back arm creases (Diagram G).

Sleeve Length

Feel for the knob at the end of your shoulder and keep a finger there. Depending on your body, it may help to raise your elbow as high as your shoulder. Place your hand on your hip; measuring with your arm bent builds in ease for your sleeve. Measure from the shoulder knob over the elbow to your wrist bone (Diagram H).

Upper Arm Width

Measure the fullest part of your arm between the shoulder and the elbow, with a thumb or a finger underneath the tape measure to make sure it is not too tight. Measure to the closest ½" (Diagram I).

Diagram D: Measure hip width.

Diagram E: Use free end of tape measure to check hipline length.

Diagram F: Measure back length from neck to waist.

Diagram G: Measure across back above arm creases.

Diagram H: Measure sleeve length from shoulder to wrist with arm bent.

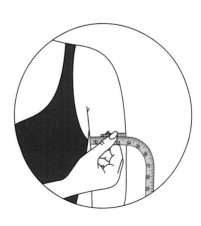

Diagram I: Measure upper arm.

Choosing Your Pattern Type

Now that you know your correct size by using the front width measurement, you have a choice of which type of pattern to buy—Misses', Petite, Juniors, Half Size, or Women's. For example, if your front width measurement is 13½", you could buy a Misses' 12, a Juniors 11, or a Half Size 12½. A complete chart of pattern size measurements by type appears on page 140, across from your Personal Fitting Chart. Use that chart and the information below to help you decide which pattern type is best for you.

Misses': These patterns are designed for women whose figures are well proportioned and well developed, who are approximately 5'5" to 5'6", and who wear a B-cup bra (*Diagram A*).

Petite: These patterns are made for women who are approximately 5'2" to 5'3" but are similarly proportioned to the Misses' figure. Bust, waist, and hip measurements are the same as those for Misses' patterns (*Diagram B*).

Juniors: Juniors patterns are designed for women who are well proportioned, short waisted, and who are about 5'1" to 5'3", with an A/B-cup bra size (*Diagram C*).

Half Size: Half Size patterns have more room allotted in the bust, the waist, and the hip than Misses' patterns, with shorter length proportions, and are made for women between 5'2" and 5'3", with a C-cup bra size. If you usually buy Half Size patterns and are comfortable with the proportions, keep doing so (*Diagram D*).

Women's: The Women's figure type is the same height as the Misses' (5'5" to 5'6") but is fuller and larger in the bust (D cup), the waist, and the hip (*Diagram E*).

Note from Nancy: Don't worry if your bust, waist, hip, or back waist length are not the same as those in the charts. In this book, I'll show you how to alter patterns easily.

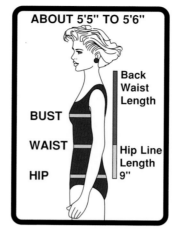

Diagram A: Misses' measurements

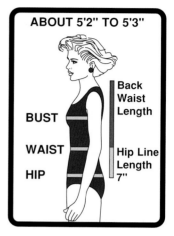

Diagram B: Petite measurements

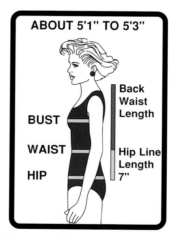

Diagram C: Juniors measurements

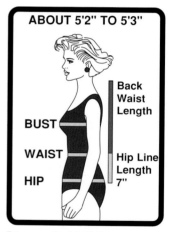

Diagram D: Half Size measurements

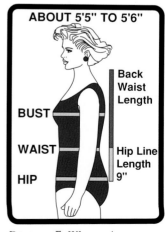

Diagram E: Women's measurements

Comparing Measurements

Now that you've determined your correct size and pattern type, and you've recorded your measurements on the Personal Fitting Chart on page 141, it's time to compare your measurements to those on the back of the pattern envelope (*Diagram*).

The four areas given on a pattern envelope are bust, waist, hip, and back waist length. Fill in the appropriate measurements in your Personal Fitting Chart. You will also need to measure your sleeve length and upper arm width, and the pattern length,

even though these measurements are not given on the pattern envelope. In subsequent chapters you will check these measurements against the paper pattern pieces.

To make the comparison easy, you will find your Personal Fitting Chart opposite the Pattern Size Chart. When you're using this book to alter a specific pattern, you may want to use a paper clip or a bookmark to help you easily locate the pages with these charts.

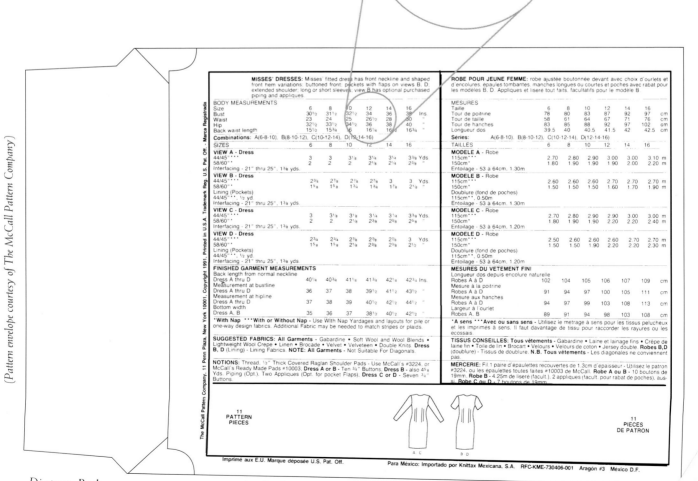

Diagram: Body measurements appear on back of pattern envelopes.

(Pattern envelope courtesy of The McCall Pattern Company)

Body Silhouettes

There's more to Fitting Finesse than just knowing the right size and the pattern group to buy. Another part is knowing which pattern styles, fabrics, and colors flatter your figure. Analyze your figure to decide which body silhouette matches yours and choose clothes to enhance it. The high fashion houses in Paris do this for their clients, and now you can do it, too!

On page 134, you will find a complete Body Silhouette Chart, specifying which pattern styles, fabrics, and colors complement each figure type. Study the chart to decide which silhouette most closely resembles yours. Record pertinent information on your Personal Fitting Chart, page 141.

Before you shop for a particular pattern, test information about your body silhouette by visiting your favorite department store or a trendy boutique and trying on garments in the styles recommended for your body silhouette. Make a photocopy of your Personal Fitting Chart and take it along as a guide.

Be sure to check out styles you haven't tried before. Analyze the styles you like to determine what makes them flattering on you—the design, the fabric, or the details? Jot these down in a notebook. Next, head for your favorite sewing center to select patterns and fabrics that flatter your figure.

Seven Types

Body silhouettes fall into seven basic categories: pear-shaped, full-busted, full-figure, long-waisted, short-waisted, petite, and slim-tall.

If you are **pear shaped**, choose clothes that seem to broaden your shoulders and balance your figure. Anything that adds fullness or draws attention to your upper body can help meet that goal. Put bright colors above the waist and use trim or jewelry with one-color outfits to draw attention to the shoulders and the upper body (*Diagram A*).

The **full-busted** body silhouette makes an upside-down triangle shape, with the largest part at the bust. To balance a full-busted silhouette, add linear emphasis below the waist with dropped waists or hip yokes. Soften the bustline with shoulder tucks or pleats (*Diagram B*).

For a **full figure**, create a slimmer look by using vertical lines to draw the eye up and down the body rather than across. Long tunic tops, loose-fitting long jackets, and one-color outfits (but not necessarily a dark color) can accomplish this goal. Remember in two-color outfits to use darker fabrics at your heaviest or fullest body part and dull textures to minimize attention to your figure's fullness (*Diagram C*).

Diagram A: Broader shoulders in garment balance pear-shaped figure.

Diagram B: Shoulder tucks add fullness without emphasizing full-busted silhouette.

Diagram C: For full figure, create slimmer look by wearing loose-fitting, long jackets.

If you are **long waisted**, choose styles that visually shorten your upper torso. Yokes, wide collars, pockets, epaulets, or lapels draw attention across the shoulders, making your upper body seem wider and shorter. Make sure your belt color matches the fabric below your waistline to visually lengthen your lower torso (*Diagram D*).

If you're **short waisted**, use dropped-waist styles and V necks to visually lengthen the upper torso in relation to the lower body. Princess styles draw the eye up and down without strictly defining your waistline. Allover prints can help balance your figure (*Diagram E*).

If you're **petite**, you can use clothing style and color to help make you appear taller. One key to doing this is to achieve a one-third to two-thirds division of your figure (either upper body to lower body or the other way around) through use of colors and design features. Short sleeves on a one-piece dress are one way to create a one-third to two-thirds proportion. A long jacket combined with a short skirt creates a two-thirds to one-third proportion. V necks, tiered layers on skirts, and short jackets all enhance a petite silhouette (*Diagram F*).

The figure type which allows the widest variety of patterns and styles is the **slim-tall** silhouette. If you have this silhouette, you have a small bone structure and are at least 5'7". You may also have an athletic build with broad shoulders and narrower bust, waist, and hips than average. Make the most of your silhouette by layering jackets, vests, blouses, and tunics. Use textured fabrics such as bulky woolens, textured tweeds, and other nubby fabrics (*Diagram G*).

Diagram D: Big collar draws eye across shoulders to help long-waisted figure.

Diagram E: Short-waisted figures need to visually lengthen upper torso.

Diagram F: Short jackets enhance a petite silhouette.

Diagram G: Slim-tall figure is ideal in that variety of styles, colors, and fabrics looks good on it.

Choosing a Classic Style

For your first fitting project, choose a classic-style blouse, skirt, dress, or jacket. By first trying the techniques I present in this book on a classic-style pattern, you will learn methods of making your clothes fit that you can then easily use on *any* style pattern.

A classic style means:

• Set-in sleeves with no dropped shoulders or extra gathering

• Shoulder seams with no yoke over the shoulders (although a decorative front or back yoke is fine)

• No excessive gathering, tucking, or pleating on the sleeves or the body

• Comfortably fitting jacket, not loose-fitting or oversize

• Straight, A-line, or bias-cut skirt without excessive fullness

Note from Nancy: I recommend you start with a pattern that is made up of a minimum number of pieces rather than a fitting-shell pattern (which results in an unfinished test garment). You can just as easily check the quality of the fit on a classic-style pattern as on a fitting shell, plus you use your precious time to add to your wardrobe.

For the most part, once you know what alterations to make on a classic-style pattern, you will automatically make those same changes on *every* pattern from that company, no matter what the style. Use your Personal Fitting Chart like a recipe for express-style fitting.

Shoulder seams without yoke

A-line skirt

Set-in sleeves

Streamlined style—no excess gathers, pleats or tucks

Comfortably fitting jacket

Pants with fitted waist

Choose pattern for classic-style garment like any of these for your first Fitting Finesse project.

ALLOWING DESIGN EASE

All patterns are designed with ease, a little extra room that gives both comfort and fashion. The amount of ease varies depending upon the style and the type of fabric for which the pattern was designed (*Diagram A*).

Design ease is the difference between the measurements on the back of the pattern, which apply to all patterns from that company, and the actual measurements of your tissue pattern, which apply only to the style you purchased.

The only time you need to check the pattern tissue measurements for the amount of design ease is when you think an oversize style may have too many inches of ease or a form-fitting style may not have enough ease for your taste.

For woven fabrics, the minimum ease requirements to ensure a garment fits comfortably without binding are:

Bust:	3" to 4"
Waist:	½" to 1"
Hip:	3" to 4"

Designers use these amounts as guidelines, varying the actual ease to give fashion and style to patterns. A loose-fitting jacket, for example, might have as much as 6" to 8" of bust ease.

Checking Design Ease

It's simple to check the design ease allowed in your pattern.

• Pin the front and back pattern pieces together at the underarm, stacking the stitching lines.

• Hold the tape measure with the 1" end in your left hand. Fold this end of the tape measure until it meets the bust measurement from the back of your pattern envelope. For example, if you are using a Misses' size 12, the bust measurement is 34".

• Position the folded end of the tape measure across the bust area, measuring from the stitching (or fold) line of the center front to the

Diagram A: Design ease is extra room in garment that gives both comfort and style.

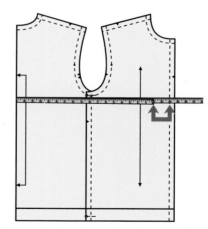

Diagram B: Stack stitching lines and double amount indicated by red arrows to get total design ease.

stitching (or fold) line of the center back (*Diagram B*).

• The gap between the 1" end of the tape measure and the stitching (or fold) line of the center back is half of the ease; double this measurement to find out the total design ease. Remember, you only need to check ease for tight- or loose-fitting styles.

Note from Nancy: Vogue and McCall's print the actual pattern width on the tissue, making the ease extremely simple to determine. McCall's also prints finished garment measurements on the back of the pattern envelope.

Learning to Pivot and Slide

You know what size you wear. You've recorded your body measurements, determined your figure silhouette, and selected a classic-style pattern. All you need now is to learn the pivot-and-slide techniques that will let you achieve Fitting Finesse.

Note from Nancy: I've been sewing since the age of 10 and have tried practically every method of changing a pattern. I've slashed and spread, folded and tucked, and added a little at the seam allowances while cutting out the pattern. Needless to say, I've had a variety of successes and failures with my initial experiments. Since I learned how to change a pattern with pivot-and-slide techniques, I haven't wavered. I know you'll have the same positive results.

Pattern designers use pivoting methods to make fashion changes. They move darts or add fullness by anchoring the basic pattern with a pin and moving the pattern in, out, and around. The pattern swings back and forth like the pendulum on a grandfather clock. Use this pivoting motion to change the pattern width (*Diagram A*).

Pattern graders use the slide motion to change pattern sizes. They slide patterns up, down, and to the side to gradually increase or decrease from one size to the next. Use this sliding motion to add or subtract length (*Diagram B*).

Pivot-and-slide techniques combine these two motions to fit a pattern simply yet accurately. You make all of the changes on a work sheet (made of waxed paper or tissue paper), keeping the original pattern intact—no more cutting and taping! By changing the pattern equally on both sides of the grain, you keep the seam and the design lines in proportion to the original pattern. Best of all, each alteration only takes five easy steps.

Organizing Your Fitting Tools

Fitting is streamlined with pivot-and-slide techniques. So are the tools you will need. Check your sewing room, desk, and kitchen for these essential tools and supplies.

• **Work sheets:** Choose waxed paper or tissue paper since you can easily see through these economical sheets. All pattern changes are made on work sheets.

Note from Nancy: When working with larger pattern pieces, you may want to tape two work sheets together or use 21"-wide pattern paper. Pattern paper comes on a roll, and it's a real time-saver!

• **Altering tools:** Use two colors of pen (black and a second color) for tissue; a pencil and a tracing wheel for waxed paper. You will need two different marks on each work sheet—the original cutting line and the changes or alterations.

If you are using waxed paper as a work sheet, a tracing wheel and a pencil make it easy to transfer darts and grain lines. Work on a padded surface, such as an extra layer of fabric, and place the waxed paper and the pattern on top. The pencil and the tracing wheel will scratch off the wax and leave two distinctive marks.

• **Basic tools:** Use a tape measure, a ruler, tape, and pins.

Getting Ready

• Cut out the front, back, and sleeve (if applicable) pattern pieces along the cutting lines. Press the pattern tissue pieces with a dry iron.

• Cut a work sheet as long as each pattern piece. Don't worry if the waxed paper isn't wide enough. The work sheet only needs to extend to the side of the pattern as much as needed for the alteration.

• Study the next page, "Reading Diagrams" and then turn to the appropriate chapter to try out Fitting Finesse!

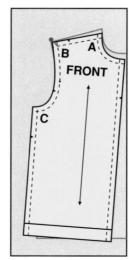

Diagram A: Using pin as anchor, pivot your pattern like pendulum of grandfather clock.

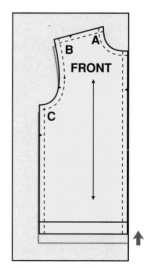

Diagram B: Slide pattern vertically or horizontally on work sheet to change size.

Reading Diagrams

This book is designed to be a resource whenever you sew. Each chapter focuses on a different area of fitting and provides detailed instructions for completing both increases and decreases at various pattern points.

At the end of the book is a handy Reference chapter containing your Personal Fitting Chart and Pants Personal Fitting Chart, along with various tables and charts that are mentioned throughout the book. Some charts that appear within chapters (including the Front Width Measurement Chart) are repeated in the Reference chapter to make them quick and easy to find.

Color Coding

Illustrations for the specific pivot-and-slide steps are color coded. Pattern pieces are always cream colored. Work sheets are always gray. Outlines of original pattern cutting lines are always dark gray. Steps being illustrated are always red. Steps you completed in an earlier illustration are always green.

Diagrams A, B, C, D, and E show how this color coding works. They illustrate the steps used to increase the width of a short sleeve (page 31).

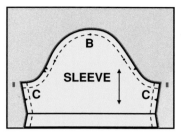

Diagram A: Outline pattern (shown in gray) and mark increase on both sides (shown in red).

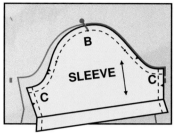

Diagram B: Pivot to 1 increase mark and trace half sleeve cap plus 1" of side seam. (First pivot step is shown in red; outline of original pattern piece is dark gray.)

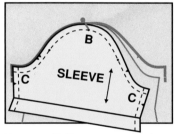

Diagram C: Pivot to second mark and trace remainder of sleeve cap. (First pivot step is now green, and second pivot step is red.)

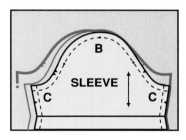

Diagram D: Slide pattern horizontally to increases and trace side seams. (Completed cap alteration is now green, and new side seam is red.)

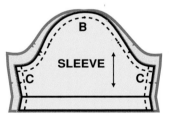

Diagram E: Completed alteration (Original pattern is cream, enlarged work sheet pattern is gray, and completed lines of new pattern are green.)

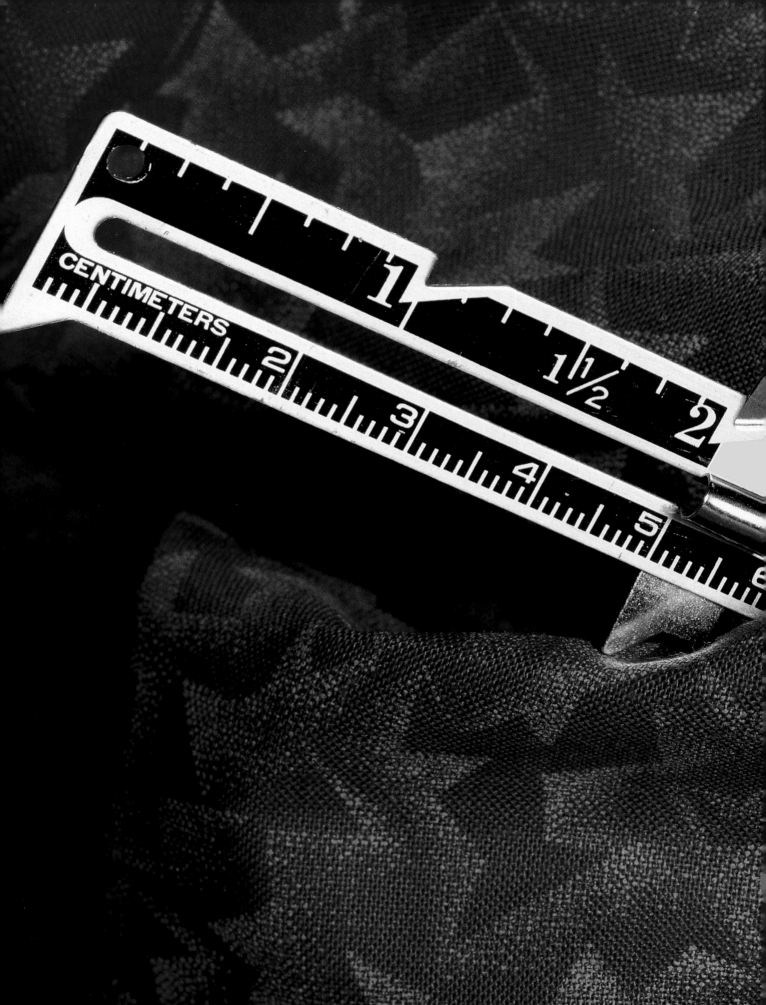

Blouse, *Dress,* and Jacket Fitting Finesse

If you must alter patterns before you sew, you're in good company. Even if your measurements correspond to those on the pattern, you may need to correct for sloping shoulders, move darts, or make other adjustments for your body's unique shape.

The first patterns were merely guides for style, which were always altered to fit individuals. Today's patterns are standardized, so it's not surprising that most of us must alter them.

Let's begin by determining which changes you need, and then you'll learn to pivot and slide your way to Fitting Finesse.

Quick Reference

PIVOT POINTS

Blouses, jackets, and dresses have the most places where you might need to make alterations, and so this is the longest chapter in the book. In fitting a skirt, you can only alter the waist, the hip, and the overall length. To fit a dress, you may need to alter at any of these points, plus you could enlarge or reduce the bust, change darts, and alter the back, the shoulders, or the sleeves.

Thank heavens for the pivot-and-slide techniques of Fitting Finesse! Five easy-to-follow steps allow you to make any changes you need. To pivot a pattern, place a pin at a specified point and swing the pattern like the pendulum of a clock.

To make pivot-and-slide instructions as clear as possible, the five basic pivot points for blouses, jackets, and dresses are coded with letters A through E. These letter codes remain the same throughout the book. The waist pivot point, for example, is always D, whether it's on a jacket, skirt, or pant pattern. Mark the following pivot points on your patterns (*see diagrams below*):

A—Point where neck and shoulder stitching lines cross

B—Point where shoulder and armhole stitching lines cross

C—Point where armhole and side seam stitching lines cross

D—Point where waist and side seam stitching lines cross

E—Point where hip and side seam stitching lines cross

The pivot points on sleeve pattern pieces match those on the armhole areas of main pattern pieces. Mark the following three pivot points on the sleeves of your patterns:

B—Point on stitching line at large dot at cap of sleeve

C—Points where armhole and underarm stitching lines cross at both sides of sleeve

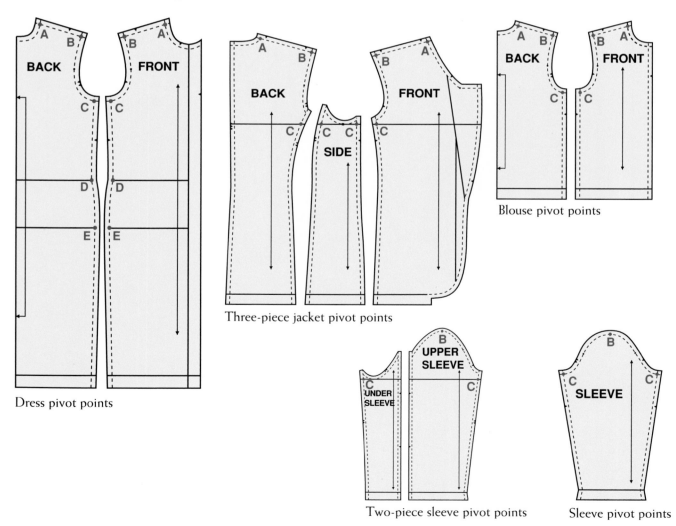

Dress pivot points

Three-piece jacket pivot points

Blouse pivot points

Two-piece sleeve pivot points

Sleeve pivot points

DRAWING REFERENCE LINES

When instructions call for extending the grain line or adding a reference line (underarm line, hip line, etc.), use a yardstick and a marking pen to draw on the pattern piece. Transfer the line to the work sheet by using a tracing wheel. Place the pattern on top of the work sheet; trace along the line. The tracing wheel points will perforate the work sheet, producing a guideline.

Grain Lines

Extend the grain line the full length of the pattern and the work sheet to make it easier to slide the pattern up and down when changing length.

Reference Lines

Reference lines should be drawn perpendicular to the grain line printed on the pattern. For a hip line, measure down from the waist line on the pattern piece the amount of your hip line length (see page 11 for how to take this measurement). For an underarm line on a three-piece jacket or a two-piece sleeve, draw the reference line so that it crosses the lowest point on the stitching line under the arm.

READING DIAGRAMS

Pivot-and-slide techniques simplify the fitting process, and the color coding makes it easy to read the diagrams. In each illustration, basic outlines are in dark gray, the step that is being demonstrated appears in red, and steps that were completed in an earlier illustration are green. The pattern is cream and work sheets are light gray.

CHOOSING PATTERNS

Be sure you are using the best pattern size for you. Instead of choosing the size based on your bust measurement, try the front width measurement (page 9). This helps you find the size with the easiest alterations necessary for your upper body.

Take all of your measurements ahead of time and record them in the Personal Fitting Chart on page 141.

If this is your first alteration project using pivot-and-slide techniques, use a classic-style pattern—one with set-in sleeves and no dropped shoulders; shoulder seams and no yoke (except a purely decorative one); no excessive gathering, tucking, or pleating on the sleeves or body; a comfortably fit (not oversize) jacket; and a straight, A-line, or bias-cut skirt without excessive fullness.

Finally, make sure you have all the tools you will need to complete the project (page 18).

Comfortably fitting jacket

Set-in sleeves

Shoulder seam without yoke

Pants with fitted waist

Streamlined style— no excess gathers, pleats, or tucks

Straight skirt

Classic-style patterns

Bust Changes

Determining Changes

Compare your bust measurement to the bust measurement for your size on the back of the pattern envelope (*Diagram A*). The difference between these two equals the amount of alteration you need to make. For example:

Actual measurement	37"
Pattern envelope	34"
Alteration	+3"

To determine how much to add to each cut edge, divide your alteration amount by four (the total number of cut edges at both side seams).

Note from Nancy: I quickly determine the alteration I need at each cut edge by creating a fraction. In this example, place the alteration amount (3") over the number of cut edges (4). Presto! The amount to add per edge is ³⁄₄"!

If you need to add more than 4" total (1" per side seam) to the bust width, see page 34 for how to use extensions.

INCREASING

1. Outline the pattern and mark the increase.

• Place the front pattern piece on a work sheet; outline the cutting lines of the pattern on the work sheet using a black marker.

• Measure the needed increase out at the underarm cutting line; mark (*Diagram B*).

2. Place a pin at pivot point B; pivot the pattern out to the increase mark. Trace the new armhole cutting line with a colored marker (*Diagram C*).

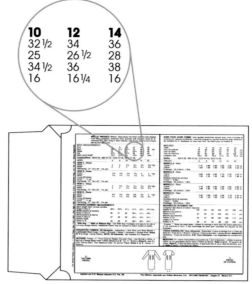

10	12	14
32½	34	36
25	26½	28
34½	36	38
16	16¼	16

Diagram A: Body measurements are printed on back of pattern envelope.

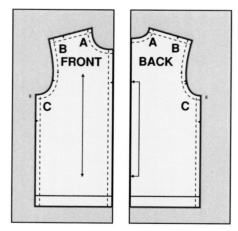

Diagram B: Outline pattern; mark.

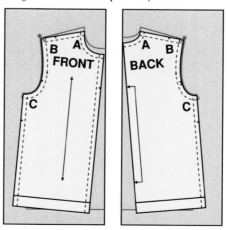

Diagram C: Pivot to increase mark; trace armhole.

Blouse without darts

3. Keeping the pattern pivoted, move the pin to pivot point C; pivot the pattern in to the original outlined waist. Trace the new cutting line between the underarm and the waist; mark the notches (*Diagram D*).

4. Match the pattern to the original outline and tape it to the work sheet. Cut out, following the new outline.

5. Repeat steps 1 through 4 on the back pattern piece (*Diagram E*).

Note from Nancy: When you place the pattern in its original position, notice the alteration. The bust width is increased, but the armhole is the same size as the original pattern. Plus your pattern is still intact.

DECREASING

1. Outline the pattern and mark the decrease.

• Place the front pattern piece on a work sheet; outline the cutting lines of the pattern.

• Measure the needed decrease in from the underarm cutting line; mark (*Diagram AA*).

2. Place a pin at pivot point B; pivot the pattern in to the decrease mark. Trace the new armhole cutting line; mark the notches (*Diagram BB*).

3. Keeping the pattern pivoted, move the pin to pivot point C; pivot the pattern out to the original waist. Trace the new cutting line between the underarm and the waist; mark the notches (*Diagram CC*).

4. Match the pattern to the original outline. Fold in the pattern sections that overlap the new outline; tape. Cut out, following the new outline.

5. Repeat steps 1 through 4 on the back pattern piece (*Diagram DD*).

Note from Nancy: When a pattern is decreased, fold back the original pattern piece so that the new cutting line is visible.

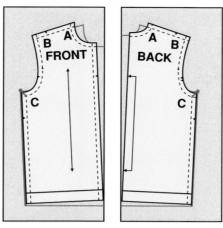

Diagram D: Pivot to waist; trace side.

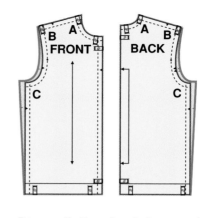

Diagram E: Completed alteration for bust increase

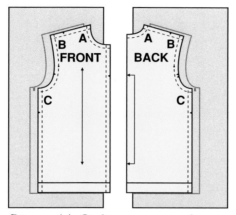

Diagram AA: Outline pattern; mark decrease.

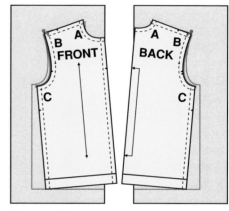

Diagram BB: Pivot to decrease mark; trace armhole.

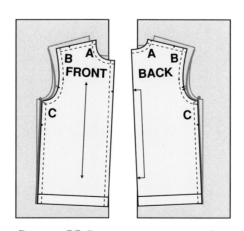

Diagram CC: Pivot to waist; trace side.

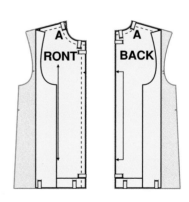

Diagram DD: Completed alteration for bust decrease

FITTING A JACKET WITH SIDE PANELS

Just when you think you've mastered fitting the bust, you come across a jacket pattern with not two but *three* main body pieces: the front, the back, and the side panel. Don't worry. Basic pivoting techniques in five easy steps still apply, with only a slight amount of fine-tuning.

Note from Nancy: We still alter only four cut edges, even though there is an extra pattern piece. The width of the side panel pattern piece remains the same.

1. Mark an underarm reference line.
• Pin the front, side panel, and back pattern pieces together at the underarm seam, stacking the stitching lines.
• Extend a line perpendicular to the grain line from the underarm of the side panel to both the front and back pattern pieces (*Diagram A*).
• Unpin the pattern pieces.

2. Outline the pattern and mark the needed increase.
• Place the front and back pattern pieces on separate work sheets; outline the pattern.
• Measure the needed increase out from the underarm cutting line on both the front and back pieces; mark (*Diagram B*). If decreasing, measure in from the cutting line.

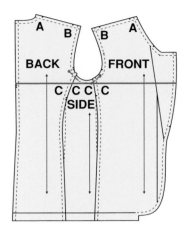

Diagram A: Pin underarm stitching lines together; draw underarm line perpendicular to grain.

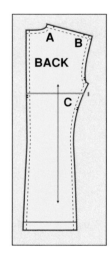
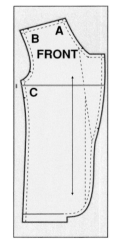

Diagram B: Outline pattern; mark increase at underarm line.

Jacket with side panels has three main body pattern pieces.

3. Pivot twice to increase the new armhole and side seam.

• On the front pattern piece, place a pin at pivot point B; pivot the pattern out to the bust increase mark. Pivot in, if decreasing. Trace the armhole and the side seams to the underarm line; mark notches (*Diagram C*).

• Keeping the pattern pivoted, move the pin to pivot point C; pivot the pattern to the outline at the hem. Trace the new underarm seam; mark the notches (*Diagram D*).

• Match the pattern to the original outline and tape. Cut out, following the new outline (*Diagram E*).

• Measure the distance between the original outline and the alteration on the front pattern piece at the armhole side seam (*Diagram F*). Record this measurement on the pattern.

4. Repeat Step 3 on the back pattern piece.

5. Alter the side panel.

• Outline the side panel pattern piece on a work sheet; extend the grain line.

• From the underarm cutting line, measure up the distance measured between the old and new cutting lines; mark.

• Slide the pattern up along the grain line to the mark. Trace the new underarm cutting line and 1" of each side seam cutting line (*Diagram G*).

Note from Nancy: When decreasing the pattern, measure down the same distance and slide the pattern along the grain line to the mark. Once you know how to increase, decreasing is the same process done in the opposite direction.

• Match the pattern to the original outline; tape. Cut out, following the new outline (*Diagram H*).

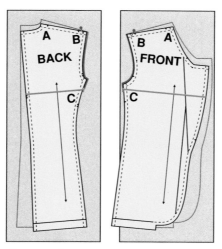
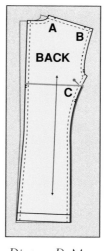
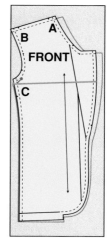

Diagram C: Pivot to increase mark; trace armhole.

Diagram D: Move pin; pivot to hem. Trace underarm cutting line.

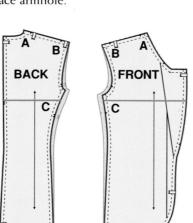
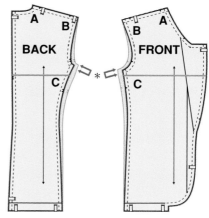

Diagram E: Completed alteration on front and back pattern pieces

Diagram F: Measure distance between old and new cutting lines (*).

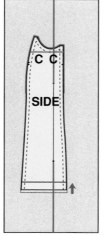

Diagram G: Slide pattern up; trace.

Diagram H: Completed alteration on side panel pattern piece

Dart Changes

MOVING THE BUST DART

This simple alteration moves the entire dart up or down without changing the length of the pattern. Determine the change by marking your bust position on the pattern.

Determining Changes

Pin the front and back pattern pieces together at the shoulder seam, stacking stitching lines.

Pin the pattern to the shoulder seam and to the center front of your undergarment.

Place a scrap of paper under the pattern to prevent the marker from bleeding onto your undergarment. On the pattern, mark the fullest part of your bust with an X (*Diagram A*).

Unpin and remove the pattern, discarding the scrap paper.

1. Determine the dart position.

• On the front pattern piece, use a ruler to extend the upper dart leg (Y) toward the center front.

• Measure the distance between this extended line and your bust point X marked on the pattern (*Diagram B*).

• Write this bust dart change measurement on the pattern and on your Personal Fitting Chart, page 141.

2. Outline the cutting lines of the pattern on a work sheet. Do not outline the side seam. Mark the amount to raise or lower the dart at the arm/side seam.

3. Create the new side seam.

• If lowering the dart, slide the pattern down at the side seam the amount noted in Step 1. Slide the pattern up by the measured amount if raising the dart. Trace the new side seam.

• Make hash marks (points Y and Z) at the side seam to mark the beginning of each dart leg (*Diagram C*).

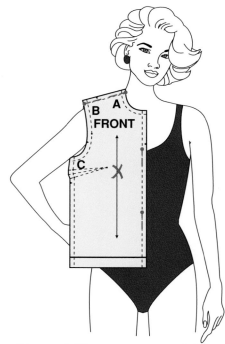

Diagram A: Try on pattern; mark bust with X.

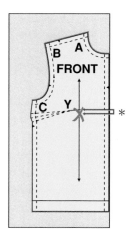

Diagram B: Measure difference from line Y and point X (*). Outline neck, shoulder, and armhole cutting lines.

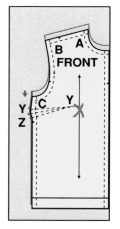

Diagram C: Slide pattern and trace; mark new dart position.

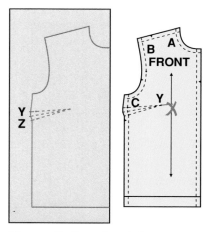

Diagram D: Completed alteration with bust dart moved

4. Trace the new dart legs.

• Place a work sheet on top of the pattern, aligning the colored lines with the pattern's side seams.

• Using the pattern piece as a guide, trace the dart legs on the work sheet (*Diagram D*). The dart is the

same size; it has simply been moved up or down, depending on the alteration you made.

5. Tape the work sheet on top of the pattern so that the changed dart is evident. Cut out, following the new outline.

ADDING A DART

If you wear a bra size larger than a B cup, you may have noticed that in clothes without darts, the waist pulls up, and bias wrinkles radiate from the underarm to the bust. Easily add a dart to avoid these problems.

1. Assemble the pattern pieces and mark the fullest part of the bust.

• Pin the front and back pattern pieces together at the shoulder seam, stacking stitching lines.

• Tape a work sheet on top of the front pattern piece below the underarm; extend the work sheet at the side and the bottom.

• Slip the pattern on, pinning its shoulder seam and its center front to your undergarment. Insert a scrap of paper under the pattern to prevent the marker from bleeding through the pattern onto your undergarment.

• Mark the pattern with an X at the fullest part of your bust (*Diagram A*).

2. Create a dart.

• At the side seam, fold the pattern and work sheet as one to form the bust dart. The fold should be deep enough to allow the center front of your pattern to hang straight. Pin the dart closed.

• Remove the pattern, leaving the dart pinned and the work sheet taped to the pattern.

• Measure and record the full depth of the dart at the side seam. The full depth is twice the folded measurement (*Diagram B*).

3. Draw the new dart's sewing and fold lines.

• Unpin the dart and draw line X on the work sheet from your bust point X to the side seam, making a line perpendicular to the grain line. Line X is merely a starting point and does not become part of the dart (*Diagram C*).

• On the work sheet, measure 1" down from line X at the underarm.

• Measure 1" from your bust point X along line X; mark, extending the line downward ½".

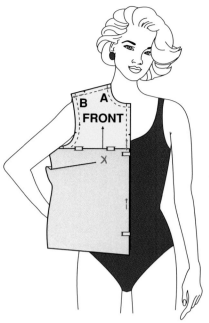

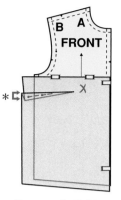

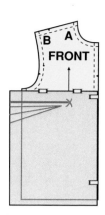

Diagram A: Pin pattern pieces together at shoulder seam. Tape work sheet on top of pattern. Try on; mark bust point (X).

Diagram B: Fold pattern to form dart; measure depth (*).

Diagram C: Draw line X.

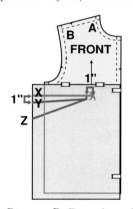

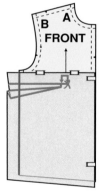

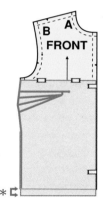

Diagram D: Draw lines from Z and Y toward X to form dart.

Diagram E: Fold pattern to form dart; draw line between underarm and waist.

Diagram F: Add depth of dart to hemline (*).

• Draw the first dart leg Y at an angle toward the fullest part of the bust, beginning at the underarm and stopping 1" before the bust point.

• Measure down from the first dart leg Y the full depth of the dart measured in Step 2; mark point Z.

• Draw a line at an angle from point Z to the end of line Y, forming the dart (*Diagram D*).

4. Draw the new side seam.

• Fold the pattern along dart leg Z to meet dart leg Y to determine the dart underlay.

• Keeping the dart folded, draw a straight line along the side seam cutting line between the pattern underarm and waist (*Diagram E*).

• Cut the pattern and the work sheet along this line and unfold. Voilà! The dart underlay and the length of the dart leg were both made at the same time.

5. On the work sheet, add the depth of the dart to the width across the bottom of the front piece (*Diagram F*). Cut out the rest of the pattern, following the new outline.

Increasing Dart Size

Misses' patterns are drafted to fit a B cup; Juniors, an A/B cup; Half Sizes, a C cup; and Women's, a D cup. Dart depth increases ½" per cup size. You may have the proportions to wear a Misses' pattern, but need a deeper dart. This method deepens the dart and automatically adds needed length to the center front. You'll be pleased to see how easy it is to make this change and how well it fits.

1. Outline the front pattern piece bottom and center front (or center cut edge).

2. Create the upper dart leg.

• Slide the pattern up ½" for each needed cup size increase. For example, to change a Misses' B-cup size to a D-cup size, slide the pattern up 1"; to change to a C-cup size, slide the pattern up ½".

• Outline the neck, shoulder, armhole, and side seams to the first dart leg Y. Place a hash mark at dart leg Y (*Diagram A*).

3. Slide the pattern down to the original lower outline of the pattern bottom. Place a hash mark at lower dart leg Z and continue to trace the side seam (*Diagram B*).

4. Draw the new dart legs.

• Match the pattern to the outline marks at the shoulder area on the work sheet; tape. Use hash mark Z made in Step 3 to draw a new lower dart leg to the original dart point.

• Treating the work sheet and the pattern as one, fold the lower dart leg to meet the top leg. Draw the new cutting line between the underarm and the second dart leg (*Diagram C*).

• Cut out the work sheet, following the new side seam cutting line. The dart underlay will be slightly wider due to the deeper dart.

5. Unfold the dart. Cut out, following the new outline (*Diagram D*).

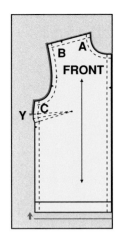

Diagram A: Slide pattern up; outline to first dart leg (Y).

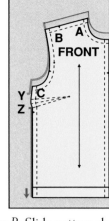

Diagram B: Slide pattern down; trace side. Mark at lower dart leg.

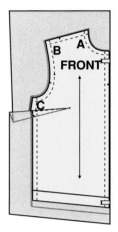

Diagram C: With dart folded, draw new cutting line between underarm and new lower dart leg.

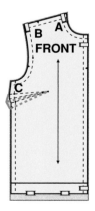

Diagram D: Completed deeper dart

Blouse with darts

Sleeve Width Changes

Sleeve changes are a snap to do once you know your sleeve and upper arm measurements. Best of all, the modified sleeve is guaranteed to fit into the armhole.

Determining Changes

Add 2" (minimum ease) to the upper arm measurement recorded on your Personal Fitting Chart (page 141).

<u>Note from Nancy:</u> Use a classic-style pattern with a basic set-in sleeve to learn these fitting techniques. Then, on other projects, you won't have to measure and check the sleeve; just add to that sleeve pattern whatever amount you used for this basic set-in sleeve.

Measure the width of the sleeve pattern at the underarm between the stitching lines (*Diagram A*).

Subtract the pattern measurement from your upper arm measurement (including ease). For example:

Arm measurement +2" ease	16"
Pattern measurement	14½"
Alteration	+1½"

Divide the increase by two (the total number of cut edges). If you need 1½", add ¾" at each cut edge of the sleeve.

To increase more than 1" per cut edge, add extensions (page 34).

INCREASING SHORT SLEEVES

1. Outline the sleeve pattern piece on a work sheet. Measure the needed increase out from the cutting lines on both sides of the pattern (in the example, ¾"); mark (*Diagram B*).

2. Place a pin at pivot point B; pivot the pattern to either increase mark. Trace half of the sleeve cap and

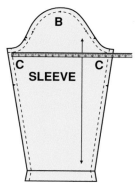

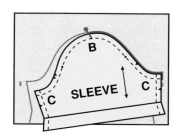

Diagram A: Measure sleeve pattern.

Diagram C: Pivot to one increase mark. Trace half of sleeve cap and 1" of side seam.

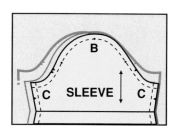

Diagram E: Slide pattern to increase; trace.

1" along the side seam. Do not draw the entire cutting line (*Diagram C*).

3. Pivot the pattern to the second increase mark; trace the other half of the sleeve cap and 1" along the side cutting line (*Diagram D*).

4. Slide the pattern to each increase mark and trace the side cutting lines.

• Remove the pin; slide the pattern horizontally along the hemline to the portion of the side cutting line traced in Step 2. Trace the new side cutting line (*Diagram E*).

• Repeat on the other side.

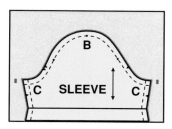

Diagram B: Outline; mark increases on both sides.

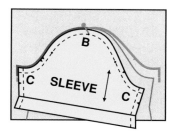

Diagram D: Pivot to second mark. Trace half of sleeve cap and 1" of side seam.

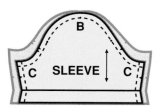

Diagram F: Completed alteration for sleeve width increase

5. Match the pattern to the original outline; tape. Cut out, following the new outline (*Diagram F*).

DECREASING SHORT SLEEVES

To decrease the width of a short sleeve, pivot the pattern in to the decrease mark; trace on the work sheet. Repeat for the opposite side. Slide the pattern horizontally to the decrease marks and finish outlining the new side cutting lines.

INCREASING LONG SLEEVES

1. Outline the sleeve pattern piece on a work sheet. Measure the needed increase out from both side seams (in the example on page 31, ¾"); mark increases at the underarms parallel to both side seams (*Diagram A*).

2. Place a pin at pivot point B; pivot the pattern to one increase mark. Trace half of the sleeve cap and 1" of the side cutting line. Do not draw the entire side cutting line (*Diagram B*).

3. Keeping the pattern pivoted, move the pin to pivot point C; pivot the pattern so that the bottom of the sleeve meets the original cutting line. Trace the new side cutting line, which gradually tapers to the original line at the hem (*Diagram C*).

4. Repeat steps 2 and 3 for the second side of the long sleeve (*Diagrams D and E*).

5. Match the pattern to the original outline; tape. Cut out, following the new outline (*Diagram F*).

<u>Note from Nancy:</u> You can decrease the width of a long sleeve by following the same steps as above, but the decrease marks will be inside the pattern cutting lines, and your work sheet will end up smaller than the pattern.

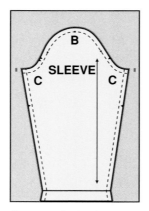

Diagram A: Outline; mark increase on each side.

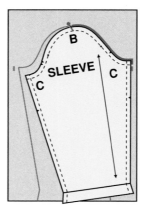

Diagram B: Pivot to one increase mark; trace.

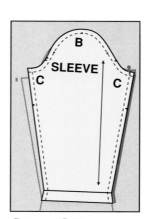

Diagram C: Pivot to bottom; trace.

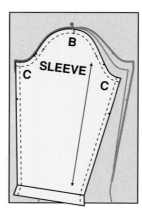

Diagram D: Pivot to second increase mark; trace.

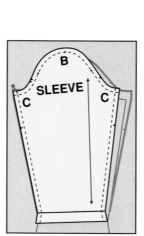

Diagram E: Pivot to bottom; trace.

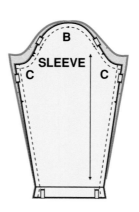

Diagram F: Completed alteration for long-sleeve width increase

Jacket with long sleeves

INCREASING TWO-PIECE SLEEVES

When increasing the width on a two-piece sleeve, all of the extra width is added to the upper sleeve. Make only a slight change in the length of the under sleeve to match the widened upper sleeve. The sleeve still fits perfectly into the armhole of your jacket.

1. Draw a reference line, outline the pattern, and mark the increase.

• Pin the sleeve pattern pieces together at the underarm seam, stacking the stitching lines. Draw a line perpendicular to the grain line from the underarm seam of the under sleeve to the upper sleeve side seam (*Diagram A*).

• Unpin the pattern pieces.

• Outline the upper sleeve pattern piece on a work sheet. Measure the needed increase out on both sides at the underarm line; mark (*Diagram B*).

2. Pivot the pattern and trace the new sleeve cap and side cutting line.

• Place a pin at pivot point B; pivot the sleeve to one increase mark. Trace the new cutting line between the cap and the increase mark (*Diagram C*).

• Keeping the pattern pivoted, move the pin to pivot point C; pivot the pattern to the original outline at the sleeve bottom. Trace the new side cutting line (*Diagram D*).

• Match the pattern to the original outline; pivot from points B and C on the other side of the sleeve.

• Match the pattern to the original outline; tape. Cut out, following the new outline.

Note from Nancy: Sometimes a small jut occurs at the new side seam near the underarm mark. Simply straighten the cutting line with a ruler.

3. Measure the distance between the original outline and the cutting line on the upper sleeve at the underarm seam (*Diagram E*). Record the measurement on the pattern and on your Personal Fitting Chart, page 141.

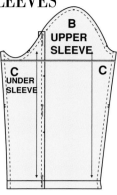

Diagram A: Pin pattern pieces together; draw underarm line.

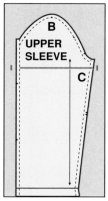

Diagram B: Outline upper sleeve; mark increase on each side.

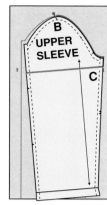

Diagram C: Pivot to increase mark; trace.

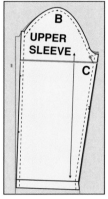

Diagram D: Pivot to sleeve bottom; trace.

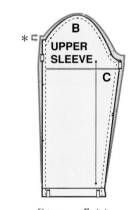

Diagram E: Measure change (*).

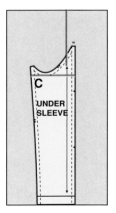

Diagram F: Outline under sleeve; mark.

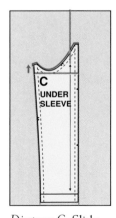

Diagram G: Slide pattern; trace.

Jacket with two-piece sleeves

4. Outline the under sleeve pattern piece on a work sheet. Extend the grain line on the pattern and transfer it to the work sheet. Measure up from the underarm cutting line the distance measured in Step 3; mark (*Diagram F*).

5. Slide the under sleeve pattern piece up along the grain line to the increase mark. Trace the underarm and 1" of each side cutting line (*Diagram G*). Match the pattern to the original outline; tape. Cut out, following the new outline.

Adding Extensions

If you need to add more than 1" per side seam at the bust or to the sleeve width, fine-tune the fit with extensions—sections added in equal amounts to the bust and to the sleeve. Extensions are added in tandem with pivoting increases. This system ensures that your armhole seams match and that your finished garment fits well and hangs nicely.

Note from Nancy: The limit of pivoting 1" per side seam only applies to the bust and the sleeve. Pivoting techniques can increase the hip and the waist by any amount—there's no limit.

When using extensions, it is important that you make *both* the sleeve and bust changes outlined below.

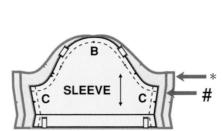

Diagram A: Completed alteration shows 1" extension increase (*) and 1" pivoting increase (#).

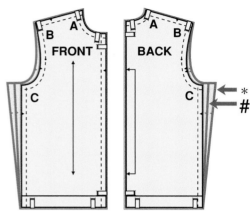

Diagram B: Finished alteration shows 1" extension increase (*) and ¼" pivoting increase (#).

Determining Sleeve Changes

If your Personal Fitting Chart on page 141 indicates that you need to add or subtract more than 4" at the bust or more than 2" at the sleeve, make the sleeve changes first. Subtract the maximum amount allowed for sleeve pivoting (2") from your needed alteration amount. The remainder will become extensions. For example:

Sleeve increase	4"
Maximum pivoting	2"
(1" per side seam)	
Needed extensions	+2"
(or 1" per side seam)	

You will have to add the same extensions to the bust area so that your sleeve armholes match your garment armholes. Use this extension amount to determine the needed bust increase.

Determining Bust Changes

For the sleeve to match the garment's underarm, the extension must be the same size at both the sleeve and the bust. Subtract the sleeve extension amount from the bust increase or decrease to determine how much to pivot. For example:

Bust increase	5"
Extension	4"
(same as for sleeves)	
Pivoting	+1"
(or ¼" per side seam)	

ADDING BUST AND SLEEVE EXTENSIONS

1. Outline the sleeve pattern piece and the garment front and back pattern pieces on work sheets.

2. Pivot the sleeve pattern piece as shown on page 31 and the bust pattern piece as shown on page 24. For the example, you would pivot 1" per side seam for the sleeve and ¼" per side seam for the bust.

3. Add extensions to the sleeve.
• Measure out 1" from the new cutting line at the underarm.

• Slide the sleeve pattern piece to the increase mark; trace the extension from the end of the pivot increase to the corner.
• On short sleeves, add the extensions the entire length of the side seam (*Diagram A*).
• On long sleeves, taper the extensions to the elbow area (middle of the underarm cutting line).

4. Add an extension to the bodice. For the example, you would measure out 1" from the new cutting line at the underarm of the front and back pattern pieces. Taper the extension to the cutting line at the waist (*Diagram B*).

5. Match the pattern pieces to the original outlines; tape. Cut out, following the new outlines.

Note from Nancy: You must always use pivoting in combination with extensions. Without the adjustments pivoting provides, an extension does not give the room you need to raise your arm.

Altering Sleeve Length

Use the grain line as a guide to add sleeve length by sliding your pattern.

Determining Changes

Measure the sleeve length on the pattern from the stitching line at the cap to the bottom stitching line (sleeve hem). Find the difference between the pattern measurement and the sleeve length measurement on your Personal Fitting Chart (page 141) to determine how much you need to lengthen or to shorten the pattern.

LENGTHENING

1. On a work sheet, outline only the lower edge of the sleeve pattern piece and 1" along each side seam.

2. Extend the grain line to the lower edge of the pattern; draw this extended grain line on the work sheet.

3. Measure the required amount up on the work sheet from the lower edge cutting line; mark (*Diagram A*).

4. Slide the pattern to trace the new cutting lines.

• Slide the pattern up, following the grain line, until the lower edge meets the lengthening mark.

• Trace the sleeve cap and the pattern sides, connecting the bottom to the original outline at the bottom edge (*Diagram B*).

5. Match the pattern to the outline on the work sheet. Fold up pattern sections that overlap the new cutting line; tape. Cut out, following the new outline (*Diagram C*).

SHORTENING

1. On a work sheet, outline only the lower edge of the sleeve pattern and 1" along each side seam.

2. Extend the grain line to the lower edge of the pattern; draw this extended grain line on the work sheet.

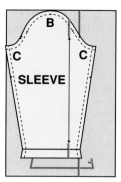

Diagram A: Outline lower edge of sleeve; extend grain line. Measure up; mark increase.

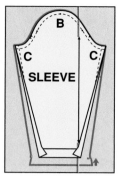

Diagram B: Slide pattern up; trace.

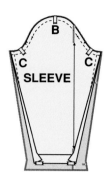

Diagram C: Completed alteration for longer sleeve

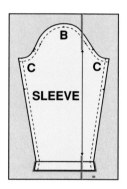

Diagram AA: Outline lower edge of sleeve; extend grain line. Measure down; mark decrease.

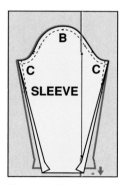

Diagram BB: Slide pattern; trace.

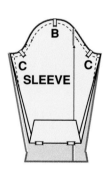

Diagram CC: Completed alteration for shorter sleeve

3. Measure down on the work sheet from the outlined lower edge the required amount; mark (*Diagram AA*).

4. Slide the pattern down, following the grain line to the decrease mark. Trace the rest of the sleeve cap and taper the pattern sides to the sleeve hem (*Diagram BB*).

5. Without moving the pattern, tape it to the work sheet, folding up pattern sections that overlap the new cutting line. Cut out the shortened sleeve pattern piece, following the new outline (*Diagram CC*).

Shoulder Changes

The key to a great fit is starting with the correct pattern size. The front width measurement (page 9) gives you a proportioned fit in the shoulder, the armhole, and the neck. That means droopy shoulders, gaping necklines, and large armholes should be fitting challenges of the past for most people. Still, you may need to fine-tune your fit in the shoulders.

Your shoulder width and shape do not change, but the shoulder width of a garment depends on the designer's preference. A jacket's padded shoulders may extend beyond your actual shoulder width, or a vest may be cut very narrow to let the shoulders of a blouse worn under it extend beyond the vest *(Diagram A)*. Your body measurements are of little value in determining the shoulder fit of many garments.

Rather than measuring your shoulders, study the picture on your pattern. Does the garment have dropped shoulders, or are the garment's shoulders supposed to sit squarely on yours?

Determining Changes

Method A—Fitting Formula: If a pattern's front width measurement is right for you, but the shoulders don't fit, make either a ¼" or ½" change. Subtract ¼" if you think your shoulders are slightly narrow or ½" for very narrow shoulders. Add ¼" to correct for slightly broad shoulders or ½" for very broad shoulders.

Note from Nancy: A ¼" or ½" decrease may not seem like a major change, but the average shoulder width is only 5". Subtracting ½" results in reducing the shoulder width by 10%.

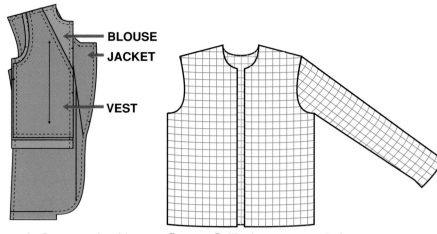

Diagram A: Compare shoulder shapes. Vest has narrowest shoulder, and jacket has widest.

Diagram B: Trial garment made from Tru-Grid

Method B–Quick Trial Garment: If you think a pattern's shoulder width needs to be changed more than ½" to fit the way you like, consider making a trial garment (also called a fitting shell).

Note from Nancy: I usually recommend against making a trial garment to test an alteration, but in the case of shoulders, where accurately measuring width is difficult, this may be helpful. Consider making a trial garment out of Tru-Grid, gridded, nonwoven fabric designed specifically for trial garments *(Diagram B)*.

• Make the trial garment as simple as possible, leaving out facings and collars. Cut out and sew together the front and back pattern pieces at the shoulder and side seams, including any darts. Set in one sleeve. Trim the ⅝" seam allowance at the neck.

• Try on the garment and pin it closed. Place a pin on the shoulder seam where you think the armhole should fall.

• Have your sewing buddy help you measure the distance between the pin and the armhole seam. That's how much you need to add or remove. Usually, you will take out or add no more than ¾" from the shoulder. As in Method A, ¼" and ½" are more common alterations.

NARROW SHOULDERS

If the sleeves hang off the shoulders, you have narrow shoulders. You can shorten the shoulder length to adjust for a narrower shoulder width and keep the armhole the same size.

1. Outline the front pattern piece on a work sheet. Measure the needed decrease amount in from the shoulder cutting line; mark *(Diagram A)*

2. Align the pattern with the outline; slide the pattern so that the shoulder cutting line meets the decrease mark.

3. Insert a pin at pivot point B; pivot the pattern out to the original underarm cutting line. Trace the new armhole *(Diagram B)*.

4. Align the pattern with the original outline; tape, leaving the armhole area free. Fold in sections that overlap the new outline. Cut out, following the new outline.

Note from Nancy: The altered armhole is the same size as the original armhole. It may appear slightly higher, but it will fit correctly.

5. Repeat steps 1 through 4 on the back pattern piece *(Diagram C)*.

Narrow shoulders cause sleeves to hang off shoulders.

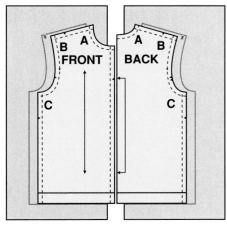

Diagram A: Outline; mark decrease.

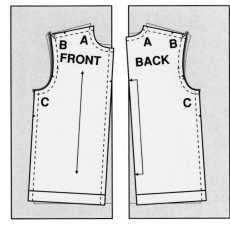

Diagram B: Pivot to underarm; trace.

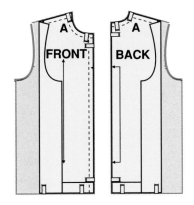

Diagram C: Completed alteration for narrow shoulders

BROAD SHOULDERS

If you have stress wrinkles at the sleeve on both the front and the back of your garments, you have broad shoulders. Having shoulders broader than the pattern is not as common a concern as narrow shoulders. You can adjust for broad shoulders by widening the shoulders of your garments. See page 36 to determine how much of a change to make.

1. Outline the front pattern piece on a work sheet. Measure the needed increase out from the shoulder; mark (*Diagram A*).

2. Slide the pattern along the shoulder seam so that the shoulder cutting line meets the increase mark; trace the wider shoulder cutting line (*Diagram B*).

3. Place a pin at pivot point B; pivot the pattern in to the original underarm cutting line. Trace the new armhole cutting line (*Diagram C*).

4. Match the pattern to the original outline and fold in sections that overlap the new cutting lines; tape. Cut out, following the new outline.

5. Repeat steps 1 through 4 on the back pattern piece (*Diagram D*).

Note from Nancy: This method adds a little to the front width measurement, too, but not enough to affect your garment's final look.

Broad shoulders cause stress wrinkles.

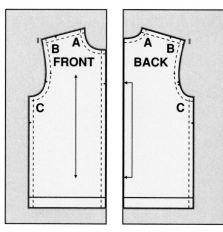

Diagram A: Outline; mark increase.

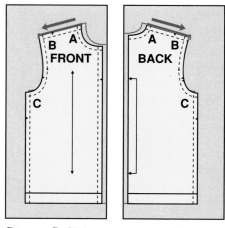

Diagram B: Slide pattern to mark; trace.

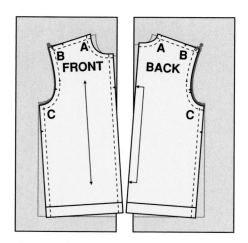

Diagram C: Pivot to underarm; trace.

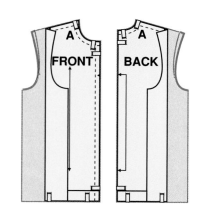

Diagram D: Completed alteration for broad shoulders

Square Shoulders

Your best cue as to whether you should make pattern changes for square shoulders is the fit of an existing garment. If your garment rides up at the neck, creating stress wrinkles at the shoulders and causing the neckline to feel too loose, you have square shoulders.

Determining Changes

As with other shoulder changes, it is difficult to measure how much to alter the pattern. Use this fitting formula to determine the alteration amount: add ¼" for slightly square shoulders or ½" for very square shoulders.

1. Outline the front pattern piece cutting lines on a work sheet. Measure ¼" or ½" up from the end of the shoulder; mark (*Diagram A*).

2. Insert a pin at pivot point A; pivot the pattern out to the increase mark. Trace the new shoulder cutting line (*Diagram B*).

3. Keeping the pattern pivoted, move the pin to pivot point B; pivot the pattern in to the original underarm outline. Trace the new armhole cutting line (*Diagram C*).

4. Match the pattern to the original outline; tape. Cut out, following the new outline.

5. Repeat steps 1 through 4 on the back pattern piece (*Diagram D*).

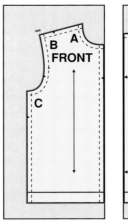

Square shoulders cause stress wrinkles at neck.

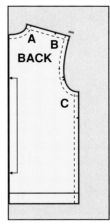

Diagram A: Outline and measure up from shoulder cutting line; mark.

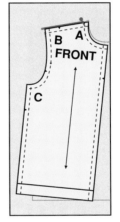
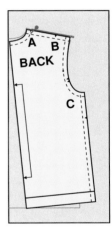
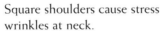

Diagram B: Pivot to mark; trace.

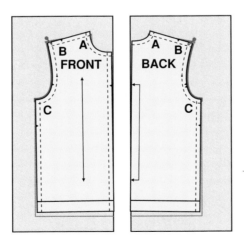

Diagram C: Pivot to underarm; trace.

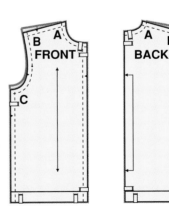

Diagram D: Completed alteration for square shoulders

SLOPING SHOULDERS

Sloping shoulders cause clothing to bind or folds to form at the underarm. Subtract ¼" for slightly sloping shoulders or ½" for very sloping shoulders.

To determine your shoulder slope, hold a yardstick parallel to the floor at your neck and look in the mirror. If the angle between the yardstick and your shoulders looks like a ski ramp, you have very sloping shoulders. Use the fitting formula on page 36 to determine alteration amounts.

1. Outline the front pattern piece on a work sheet. Measure down ¼" or ½" from the end of the shoulder cutting line; mark (*Diagram A*).

2. Place a pin at pivot point A; pivot the pattern down to the decrease mark. Trace the new shoulder cutting line (*Diagram B*).

3. Keeping the pattern pivoted, move the pin to pivot point B; pivot in to the original underarm outline. Trace the new armhole (*Diagram C*).

4. Match the pattern to the original outline and fold in the sections that overlap the new outline; tape. Cut out, following the new outline.

5. Repeat steps 1 through 4 on the back pattern piece (*Diagram D*).

Note from Nancy: The new pattern armhole slopes at a greater angle to match your body shape. This prevents the garment from binding at the underarms and eliminates folds caused by sloping shoulders.

To see how much shoulders slope, hold yardstick at neck. If angle looks like ski ramp, you have very sloping shoulders.

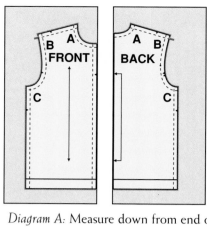

Diagram A: Measure down from end of shoulder cutting line; mark.

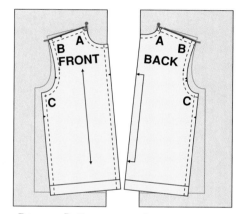

Diagram B: Pivot to mark; trace.

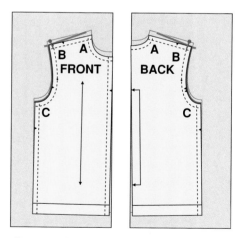

Diagram C: Pivot to underarm; trace.

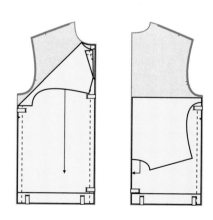

Diagram D: Completed alteration for sloping shoulders

ONE SHOULDER LOWER THAN THE OTHER

It is fairly common to have one shoulder lower than the other. In this instance, alter the pattern and the fabric *after* cutting out the pattern.

• Cut the front and back pattern pieces from your fabric without making any shoulder alterations. Unpin the pattern pieces from the fabric.

• Make sloping shoulder changes on work sheets, following the steps shown on page 40.

• On the *right* (not wrong) side of your fabric, match the work sheet pattern to the fabric *only on the side that corresponds to the sloping shoulder*. Double-check before you cut to be sure you cut the correct shoulder (*Diagram E*). Recut both the front and the back of your garment, using the work sheet as a cutting guide.

Bias wrinkles on only one side indicate that only one shoulder slopes.

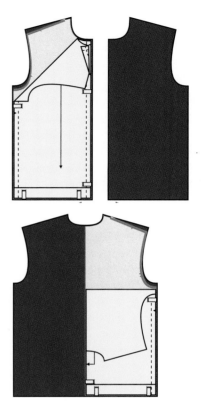

Diagram E: Match altered work sheet on *right* (not wrong) side of fabric only on the sloping shoulder side.

Back Changes

ADDING FULLNESS

A common fitting complaint with a ready-made or a sewn garment is tightness across the back. Many of us buy a larger pattern size just to improve the fit across the back only to discover that we then have a poor fit through the neck and the shoulders. Here is a way to add room across the back without purchasing a larger size.

Determining Changes

If you have already added an increase at the bust, you may not need to change your pattern to add back fullness. When you pivot, half of any amount added to the bust is automatically added to the back width. For example, if you add 1" at each side seam to increase the bust, the back width increases ½" per side seam or a total of 1" (*Diagram A*).

If you did not increase the bust, or if you need even more back width, measure your pattern to determine the amount to add.

• Add 1½" (standard ease) to the back width measurement recorded on your Personal Fitting Chart (page 141).

• Mark this measurement on your tape measure with your thumbnail. Fold the 1" end of your tape measure to this mark.

• Measure from the center back of your pattern across to the dot at the center of the armhole stitching line. Remember, if you increased the bust, you should be measuring your altered pattern.

• The distance between the 1" end of the tape measure and the armhole stitching line is the amount you need to add across the back pattern piece (*Diagram B*).

Tightness across the back causes horizontal pull wrinkles.

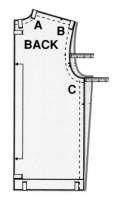

Diagram A: 1" increase at bustline equals ½" increase across back.

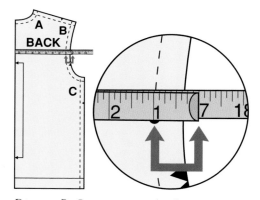

Diagram B: Compare your back measurement to pattern measurement; determine amount to add.

• Add the same increase at the center of the armhole and at the underarm to give the needed width for a broad back.

1. Outline the back pattern piece on a work sheet. Add pivot point BB at the center of the armhole. Measure out the needed increase from both the center of the armhole and the underarm cutting line; mark (*Diagram C*).

Note from Nancy: This is the only time you add in two places in one procedure.

2. Place a pin at pivot point B; pivot the pattern out to the first increase mark at the center mark on your work sheet. Trace the new armhole to the center mark on the work sheet (*Diagram D*).

3. Keeping the pattern pivoted, move the pin to pivot point BB; pivot the pattern out to the increase mark at the underarm. Trace the remaining armhole section (*Diagram E*).

4. Keeping the pattern pivoted, move the pin to pivot point C; pivot the pattern in to the original waistline. Trace the new cutting line at the side seam (*Diagram F*).

5. Match the pattern to the original outline; tape. Cut out, following the new outline (*Diagram G*).

Note from Nancy: The new armhole cutting line is not as C-shaped as the original pattern, but it is the same length. You do not have to make any alterations to the front pattern piece because the back side seam did not change in length.

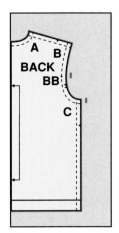

Diagram C: Outline; add pivot point BB. Mark increases at center of armhole and at underarm.

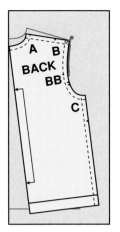

Diagram D: Pivot to armhole center; trace armhole to center mark.

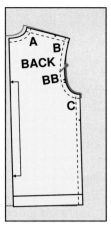

Diagram E: Pivot to underarm; trace remainder of armhole.

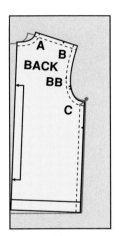

Diagram F: Pivot to waist; trace.

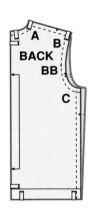

Diagram G: Completed alteration for adding back fullness

CURVED BACK

For people with a curved back or rounded shoulders, the waist length of the back pattern piece needs to be longer. Check the back pattern piece to see if the waist length is marked lower than on the front.

Determining Changes

Find your back length measurement on your Personal Fitting Chart (page 141). Compare your measurement to the measurement printed on the back of the pattern envelope. If the difference is ½" or more, alter the back pattern piece (*Diagram A*).

1. Outline the back pattern piece on a work sheet. Measure the needed length up from the neck cutting line at the center back; mark (*Diagram B*).

2. Slide the pattern up to the increase mark. Trace the longer center back and neck cutting lines (*Diagram C*).

3. Keeping the pattern in a raised position, place a pin at pivot point A; pivot the pattern to the original outline at the end of the shoulder. Trace the new shoulder cutting line (*Diagram D*).

4. Match the pattern to the original outline; tape. Cut out, following the new outline (*Diagram E*).

5. If the pattern has a shoulder dart, extend the dart legs to meet the new shoulder cutting line. Longer shoulder darts are needed for rounded shoulders (*Diagram F*).

• If the pattern doesn't have a shoulder dart, the back shoulder seam will be longer. When stitching the shoulder seams, ease the back shoulder seam to fit the front shoulder seam.

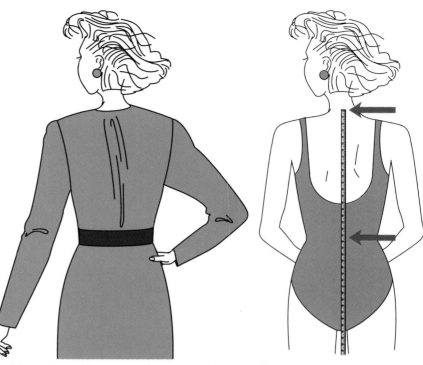

Vertical wrinkles occur when garment's back waist length is too short.

Diagram A: Back waist length is from base of neck to waist.

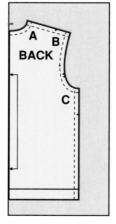

Diagram B: Outline; mark.

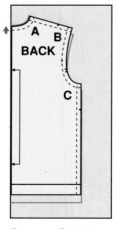

Diagram C: Slide pattern up; trace.

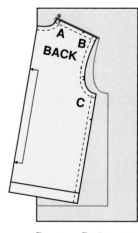

Diagram D: Pivot to shoulder end; trace.

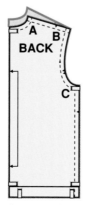

Diagram E: Completed alteration for curved back

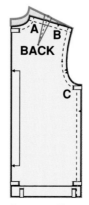

Diagram F: Draw longer dart legs.

SWAYBACK

The back pattern piece needs to be shorter for people with a swayback or very erect posture. Wrinkles that gather at the back waist indicate that the back waist length is too long.

See "Horizontal Fold Wrinkles" on page 122 to correct wrinkles below a skirt's waistband caused by a swayback.

Determining Changes

Take the back length measurement from your Personal Fitting Chart (page 141) and compare it to the one printed for your size on the back of the pattern envelope. If the difference is ½" or more, alter the back pattern piece.

1. Outline the back pattern piece on a work sheet. Measure the needed decrease down from the cutting line at the center back; mark (*Diagram A*).

2. Slide the pattern down to the decrease mark. Trace the new neckline (*Diagram B*).

3. Keeping the pattern in a lowered position, place a pin at pivot point A; pivot the pattern to the original outline at the end of the shoulder seam. Trace the new shoulder cutting line (*Diagram C*).

4. Match the pattern to the original outline; tape. Fold in the pattern sections that overlap the new outline.

5. Cut out, following the new outline (*Diagram D*).

Note from Nancy: Only the back pattern piece needs to be pivoted at the neck to correct for a curved back or for a swayback. With this method the back side seams remain the same length as the front side seams and the neckline does not change, so the collar fits the altered pattern.

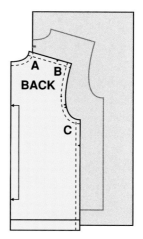

Horizontal wrinkles occur when garment's back waist length is too long.

Diagram A: Outline; mark decrease.

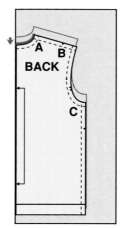

Diagram B: Slide pattern down; trace.

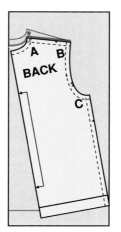

Diagram C: Pivot to shoulder seam at armhole; trace shoulder.

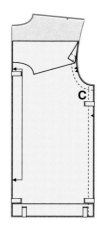

Diagram D: Completed alteration for swayback

Waist Changes

Dress and jacket alterations are essentially an expansion on blouse techniques. To alter a jacket or dress waist, you still use five easy Fitting Finesse steps, but first you need to make some calculations.

Determining Changes

Compare your waist measurement to the waist measurement for your size on the back of the pattern envelope. The difference between these two measurements equals the alteration you need to make. For example:

Actual measurement	29"
Pattern envelope	27"
Alteration	+2"

Divide the alteration amount by four (the total number of cut edges at both side seams). In the example, you would add ½" to each cut edge.

INCREASING A FITTED WAIST

1. Outline the front pattern piece on a work sheet.

2. Measure the needed increase out from the waist; mark *(Diagram A)*.

3. Place a pin at pivot point C; pivot the pattern out to the increase mark. Trace the new cutting line *(Diagram B)*.

4. Match the pattern to the original outline; tape. Cut out, following the new outline.

5. Repeat steps 1 through 4 on the back pattern piece *(Diagram C)*.

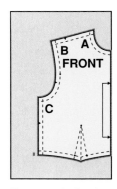
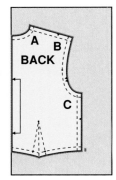

Diagram A: Outline; mark increase.

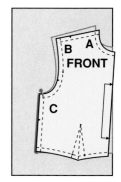
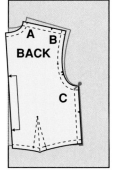

Diagram B: Pivot to mark; trace.

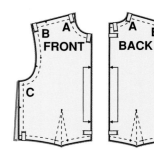

Diagram C: Completed alteration for increasing fitted waist

Dress with fitted waist

DECREASING A FITTED WAIST

1. Outline the front pattern piece on a work sheet.

2. Measure the needed decrease in from the waist; mark (*Diagram A*).

3. Place a pin at pivot point C; pivot the pattern in to the decrease mark. Trace the new cutting line (*Diagram B*).

4. Match the pattern to the original outline; tape. Fold in the pattern sections that overlap the new outline. Cut out, following the new outline.

5. Repeat steps 1 through 4 on the back pattern piece.

ALTERING A ONE-PIECE DRESS

To increase the waist on a one-piece dress, simply draw a line from the underarm to the hipline (*Diagram AA*). Use the hipline length you recorded in your Personal Fitting Chart on page 141.

If your waist is smaller than the pattern measurement, do not alter the pattern for a one-piece dress, since the waist is not fitted.

Note from Nancy: Avoid over-fitting your patterns. It isn't necessary to be exact to within 1/8" nor to remove every wrinkle. Over-fitting can be exasperating and can take the joy out of sewing.

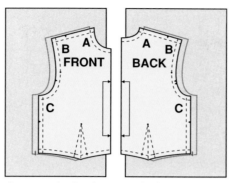

Diagram A: Outline; mark decrease.

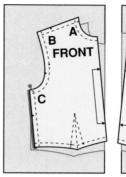

Diagram B: Pivot to mark; trace.

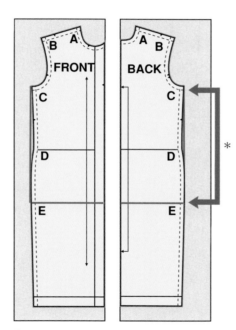

Diagram AA: Draw a line from underarm to hipline.

One-piece dress

Hip Changes

Determining Changes

Compare the hip measurement on your Personal Fitting Chart (page 141) to the hip measurement for your size on the back of the pattern envelope. The difference between the two equals the alteration you need to make. For example:

Actual measurement	40"
Pattern envelope	36"
Alteration	+4"

Divide the alteration by four (the total number of cut edges). In the example, 1" needs to be added to each side of the pattern.

ALTERING A ONE-PIECE DRESS

1. Outline the pattern and mark.
• Outline the front pattern piece on a work sheet.
• Using your hip length measurement, draw a hipline perpendicular to the grain line.
• Measure the needed increase out from the hipline; mark.
• Measure the same increase out from the side seam cutting line at the lower edge of the dress; mark (*Diagram A*). For a decrease, measure in at the hip and the hem.

2. Place a pin at pivot point C; pivot the pattern to the mark at the hip. Trace the new cutting line between the underarm and the hip (*Diagram B*).

3. Keeping the pattern pivoted, move the pin to pivot point E; pivot the pattern to the mark at the hem. Trace between the hip and hem (*Diagram C*).

4. Match the pattern to the original outline; tape. If decreasing, fold in the pattern sections that overlap the new outline. Cut out, following the new outline.

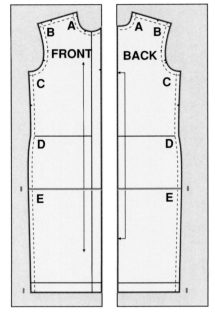

Diagram A: Outline; mark increases at hip and hem.

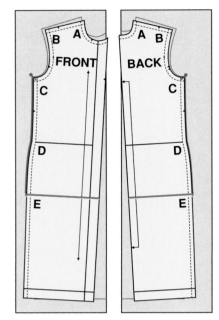

Diagram B: Pivot to hip; trace.

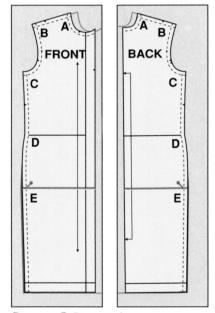

Diagram C: Pivot to hem; trace.

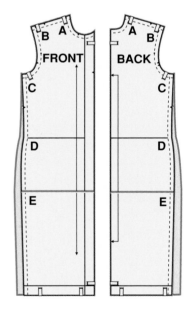

Diagram D: Completed alteration for increased hip on one-piece dress

5. Repeat steps 1 through 4 on the back pattern piece (*Diagram D*).

ALTERING A THREE-PIECE JACKET

For a three-piece jacket, you alter the front and back pattern pieces but not the side panel. This involves four cut edges, so you can use the same hip alteration amount as for a one-piece dress (page 48).

1. Outline the pattern and mark.

• Outline the front and back pattern pieces on work sheets.

• Using your hip length measurement, draw a hipline perpendicular to the grain line on each pattern piece.

• Measure the needed increase out from the hipline on each pattern piece; mark (*Diagram A*). For a decrease, measure in from the hipline.

Note from Nancy: Since the hipline and the hemline are practically at the same area on a jacket, use only one mark.

2. Place a pin at pivot point C of the front pattern piece; pivot the pattern out to the hip increase mark. If decreasing, pivot in.

3. Trace the new cutting line between the underarm and the hem (*Diagram B*).

4. Match the pattern piece to the original outline; tape. If decreasing, fold in the pattern sections that overlap the new outline. Cut out, following the new outline.

5. Repeat Step 4 on the back pattern piece (*Diagram C*).

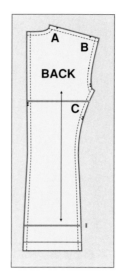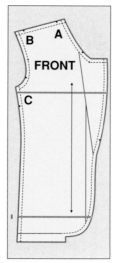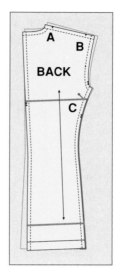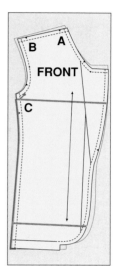

Diagram A: Outline; draw hipline perpendicular to grain line. Mark increase.

Diagram B: Pivot to mark; trace.

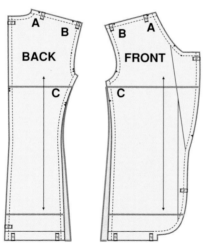

Diagram C: Completed alteration on a three-piece jacket

Three-piece jacket

Hem Changes

Use sliding techniques to change the pattern length. To keep your pattern proportional, extend the grain line or a line perpendicular to the grain and use it as a guide when sliding your pattern up, down, right, or left.

Determining Changes

Pin the front and back pattern pieces together at the shoulder seams, stacking stitching lines.

Note from Nancy: If the pattern has a stylized horizontal seam at the hip or under the bust, pin those pattern pieces together to achieve the total length of the pattern.

Pin the front pattern piece's shoulder seam and center front to your undergarment. Mark your waistline at the front and the back with your sewing buddy's help.

Walk the pattern down your figure, pinch the pattern at the desired length, and mark it with a pencil (*Diagram A*). Unpin the pattern.

Using the hem allowance printed near the pattern's hem cutting line, draw a new hemline parallel to the cutting line. Measure from your hemline to the pattern's hemline and use this amount to lengthen or to shorten the garment. Mark the new hemline on the front and back pattern pieces.

Lengthening

1. On a work sheet, outline only the bottom cutting line and 1" along the side seam and the center front of the front pattern piece. Extend the grain line on the pattern; transfer it to the work sheet. Measure the needed amount up from the bottom cutting line; mark (*Diagram B*).

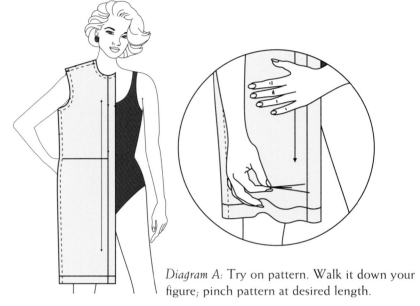

Diagram A: Try on pattern. Walk it down your figure; pinch pattern at desired length.

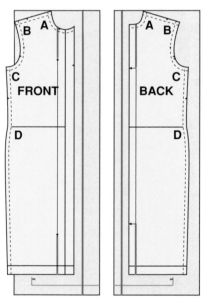

Diagram B: Outline hem; extend grain line. Mark increase.

Note from Nancy: I use a tracing wheel to trace the grain line on the pattern, so it automatically transfers through the pattern piece to the work sheet below. An alternate method is to fold the pattern along the grain line, match the traced lower edge on the work sheet to the pattern's edge, and trace along the fold line.

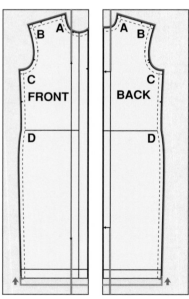

Diagram C: Slide pattern up; trace.

2. Slide the pattern up, following the grain line to the increase mark.

3. Trace the rest of the pattern (*Diagram C*).

4. Without moving the pattern, tape it to the work sheet. Cut out, following the new outline.

5. Repeat steps 1 through 4 on the back pattern piece (*Diagram D*).

SHORTENING

1. Outline only the bottom cutting line and 1" along the side seam and the center front of the front pattern piece on a work sheet. Extend the grain line on the pattern; transfer it to the work sheet. Measure the needed amount down from the bottom cutting line; mark (*Diagram AA*).

2. Slide the pattern down, following the grain line to the decrease mark.

3. Trace the rest of the pattern (*Diagram BB*).

4. Without moving the pattern, tape it to the work sheet, folding up the pattern sections that overlap the new cutting line. Cut out, following the new outline.

5. Repeat steps 1 through 4 on the back pattern piece (*Diagram CC*).

Note from Nancy: I have not given every possible alteration in this book. However, you can use the basic techniques presented to alter a wide range of garments. In the next chapter, I go beyond basic alterations to show you how to fit stylized patterns.

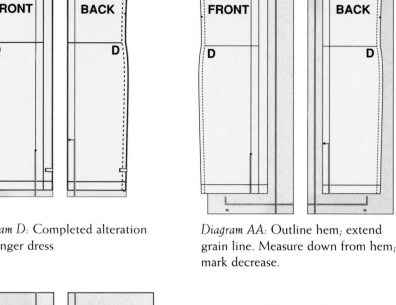

Diagram D: Completed alteration for longer dress

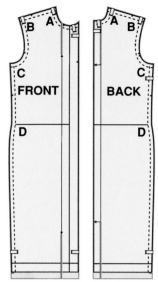

Diagram AA: Outline hem; extend grain line. Measure down from hem; mark decrease.

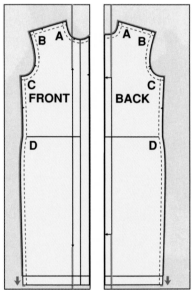

Diagram BB: Slide pattern down; trace.

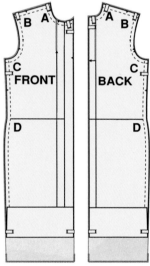

Diagram CC: Completed alteration for shorter dress

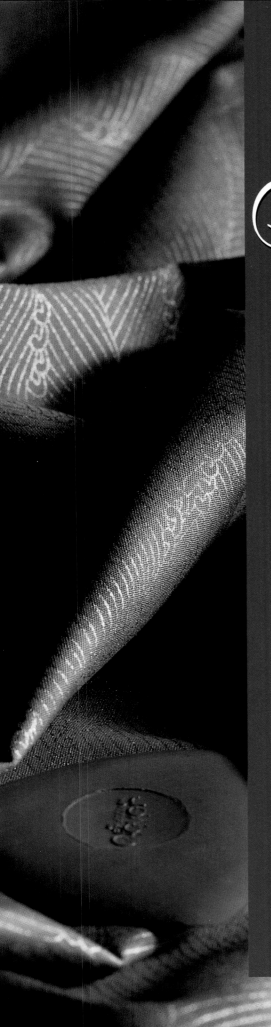

Shortcuts and Specialized Fitting

Fitting a classic-style pattern with finesse is simple, as you've seen in the first two chapters. But suppose you want to sew a jacket with raglan sleeves, a dress with princess-style seam lines, or a blouse with a yoke.

Altering stylized patterns has been a challenge, but pivot-and-slide techniques make it easy to change specialty patterns and still maintain the integrity of garments' design lines. Using key measurements from your Personal Fitting Chart on page 141, you can quickly and accurately fit patterns with stylized features.

PIVOT POINTS

To pivot a pattern, place a pin at a specific point and swing the pattern like the pendulum on a clock. On stylized patterns, these pivot points are comparable to the ones on a classic-style blouse, dress, or jacket pattern. You will mark these on a stylized pattern by using a classic-style pattern as a template. Those five basic pivot points (shown on the diagrams below) are:

A—Point where neck and shoulder stitching lines cross

B—Point where shoulder and armhole stitching lines cross

C—Point where armhole and side seam stitching lines cross

D—Point where waist and side seam stitching lines cross

E—Point where hip and side seam stitching lines cross

In addition, classic-style sleeves have the following pivot points, which match corresponding pivot points on the main pattern pieces:

B—Point on stitching line at large dot at cap of sleeve

C—Points where armhole and underarm stitching lines cross at both sides of sleeve

Be sure to read the basic instructions in "Blouse, Dress, and Jacket Fitting Finesse" beginning on page 20 before using the more advanced techniques in this chapter. Remember that red lines in the illustrations indicate changes being made, and green lines represent changes completed in an earlier step.

Drawing the Underarm Reference Line

When a pattern has multiple body pieces (a three-piece jacket, for example), use an underarm line to locate pivot point C. Pin all the pattern body pieces together at the underarm, stacking the stitching lines. Mark the underarm at the seam and draw a line perpendicular to the grain line across all the pattern pieces.

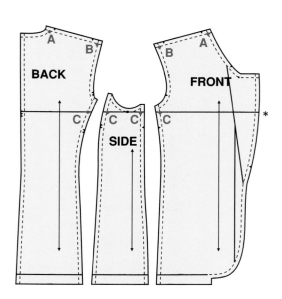

Three-piece jacket pivot points with underarm line drawn (*)

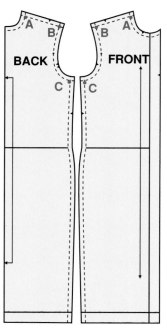

Dress pivot points

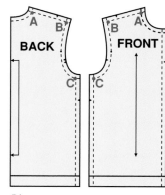

Blouse pivot points

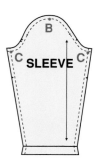

Sleeve pivot points

Altering Dolman-Sleeve and Dropped-Shoulder Patterns

Pivoting techniques make altering dolman-sleeve and dropped-shoulder patterns easy. In these styles, the sleeve or part of the sleeve is already attached to the front and back pattern pieces, so you must mark the armhole placement on these stylized patterns before altering.

The steps given in this section apply to both styles. Since the armhole seam on a dropped-shoulder pattern stays the same, you only need to alter the bodice pattern pieces, not the sleeve pattern piece.

Preparing the Pattern

• Place a classic pattern (with a basic armhole shape) on top of the stylized pattern (with dolman sleeves or dropped shoulders). Match the waists and the center fronts; the neckline and the shoulder areas do not need to match.

• Trace the armhole shape directly onto the stylized pattern. The stylized pattern will probably be larger than the classic blouse pattern, since each of these styles usually allows more ease than a classic-style pattern (Diagrams A and B).

• Remove the classic blouse pattern and put it away.

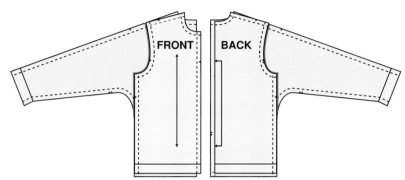

Diagram A: Position classic-style pattern on top of dolman-sleeve pattern; outline armholes and side seams.

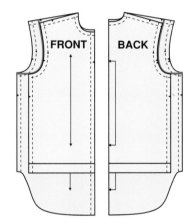

Diagram B: Position classic-style pattern on top of dropped-shoulder pattern; outline armholes.

Dropped-shoulder style (left) and dolman-sleeve style (right)

INCREASING THE BUST

Note from Nancy: The same steps are used for a dropped-shoulder pattern as for a pattern with dolman sleeves. The only difference is that the dropped-shoulder pattern sleeve is short in comparison to the dolman sleeve. Since the sleeve will not change, you only need to alter the bodice front and back pattern pieces. The changes for the dropped-shoulder pattern are basically the same as the dolman alterations in the illustrations.

1. Transfer pivot points to the specialized pattern from a classic-style pattern as shown on page 55. Outline the revised stylized pattern on the work sheet. Measure out the needed increase at the underarm area; mark (*Diagram A*).

2. Pivot and trace the new sleeve.
- Place a pin at pivot point B where the armhole line drawn from the classic-style pattern and the stitching line intersect.
- Pivot the pattern out to the increase mark.
- Trace the entire sleeve or the dropped shoulder to the increase mark (*Diagram B*).

3. Keeping the pattern pivoted, move the pin to the stylized pattern's pivot point C; pivot the pattern to the waist. Trace the new side cutting line (*Diagram C*).

4. Match the pattern to the original outline; tape. Fold in the pattern sections that overlap the new outline. Cut out, following the new outline.

5. Repeat steps 1 through 4 on the back pattern piece (*Diagram D*).

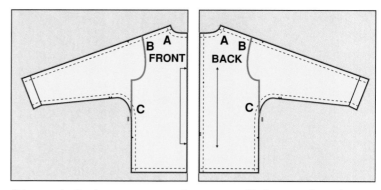

Diagram A: Outline pattern; mark increase. (Dolman style is shown.)

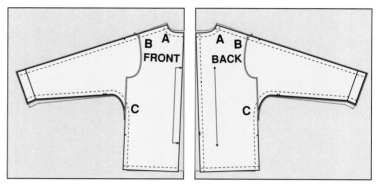

Diagram B: Pivot pattern to mark; trace entire sleeve.

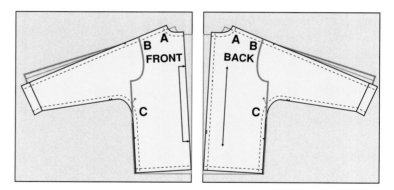

Diagram C: Pivot pattern to waist; trace side cutting line.

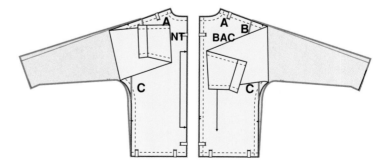

Diagram D: Completed alteration for increasing bust on dolman-sleeve pattern

DECREASING THE BUST

1. Transfer pivot points to the specialized pattern from a classic-style pattern as shown on page 55. Outline the revised stylized pattern on the work sheet. Measure in the needed decrease at the underarm area; mark *(Diagram A)*.

2. Pivot and trace the new sleeve.

• Place a pin at pivot point B where the line drawn from the stylized pattern and the stitching line intersect.

• Pivot the pattern in to the decrease mark.

• Trace the entire sleeve or the dropped shoulder to the decrease mark *(Diagram B)*.

3. Keeping the pattern pivoted, move the pin to the stylized pattern's pivot point C; pivot the pattern to the waist. Trace the new side cutting line *(Diagram C)*.

4. Match the pattern to the original outline; tape it to the work sheet. Fold in the pattern sections that overlap the new outline. Cut out, following the new outline.

5. Repeat steps 1 through 4 on the back pattern piece *(Diagram D)*.

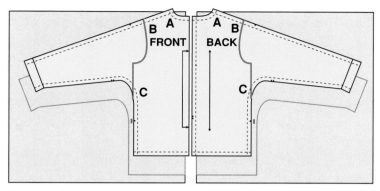

Diagram A: Outline; mark decrease. (Dolman style is shown.)

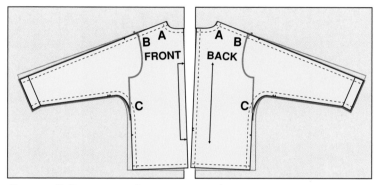

Diagram B: Pivot to mark; trace entire sleeve.

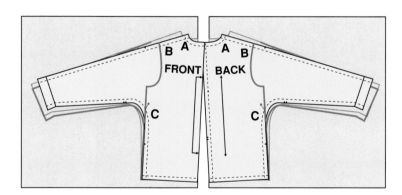

Diagram C: Pivot to waist; trace side cutting line.

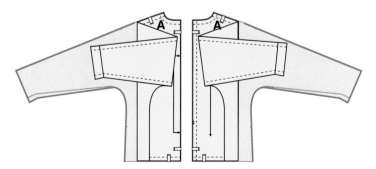

Diagram D: Completed alteration for decreasing bust on dolman-sleeve pattern

Altering Raglan-Sleeve Patterns

A top or a dress with raglan sleeves has attractive diagonal lines, a look that is flattering to many figures. It's an easy-to-sew style with straight seams in the sleeve area instead of a rounded armhole shape. Altering a pattern with raglan sleeves is very much like altering a classic-style pattern, with a few changes in the pivot points.

Marking Pivot Points

Mark the following pivot points on your raglan-sleeve pattern:

A—Point where neck and shoulder stitching lines cross

C—Point where armhole and side seam stitching lines cross

INCREASING THE BUST

1. Outline the front pattern on a work sheet. Measure out the needed increase at the underarm area; mark (*Diagram A*).

2. Place a pin at pivot point A; pivot the pattern out to the increase mark. Trace the new armhole cutting line (*Diagram B*).

3. Keeping the pattern pivoted, move the pin to pivot point C; pivot the pattern to the waist. Trace the new side cutting line (*Diagram C*).

4. Match the pattern to the original outline; tape. Cut out, following the new outline.

5. Repeat steps 1 through 4 on the back pattern piece (*Diagram D*).

DECREASING THE BUST

1. Outline the front pattern piece on a work sheet. Measure in the needed decrease at the underarm area; mark (*Diagram AA*).

2. Place a pin at pivot point A; pivot the pattern in to the decrease mark. Trace the new armhole cutting line (*Diagram BB*).

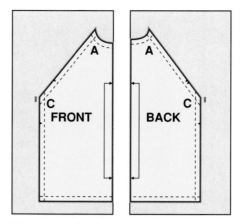

Diagram A: Outline; mark increase.

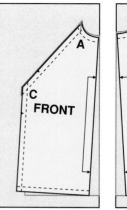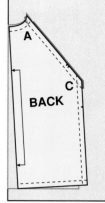

Diagram B: Pivot to mark; trace new armhole cutting line.

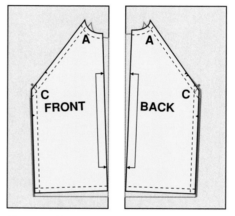

Diagram C: Pivot to waist; trace side cutting line.

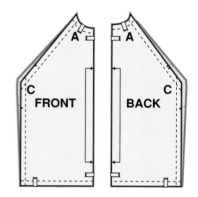

Diagram D: Completed alteration to increase bust on raglan-sleeve pattern

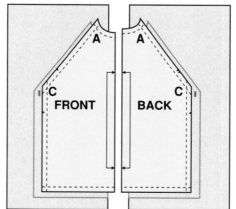

Diagram AA: Outline; mark decrease.

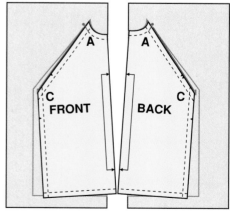

Diagram BB: Pivot to mark; trace new armhole cutting line.

3. Keeping the pattern pivoted, move the pin to pivot point C; pivot the pattern to the original waist outline. Trace the new side cutting line (*Diagram CC*).

4. Match the pattern to the original outline; tape. Fold in the pattern sections that overlap the new outline. Cut out, following the new outline.

5. Repeat steps 1 through 4 on the back pattern piece (*Diagram DD*).

INCREASING SLEEVE WIDTH

Raglan-sleeve alterations are similar to set-in sleeve changes. The only differences are that a raglan sleeve has two pieces, and each piece is pivoted at the neck edge instead of at a sleeve cap dot.

1. Outline one piece of the sleeve pattern on the work sheet. Measure out the needed increase at the underarm, parallel to the side seam; mark (*Diagram A*).

2. Place a pin at pivot point A; pivot the pattern out to the increase mark. Trace the raglan armhole and 1" of the side cutting line (*Diagram B*).

3. Keeping the pattern pivoted, move the pin to pivot point C; pivot the pattern to the original hem outline. Trace the new underarm cutting line (*Diagram C*).

4. Match the pattern to the original outline; tape. Cut out, following the new outline.

5. Repeat steps 1 through 4 on the second raglan sleeve pattern piece (*Diagram D*).

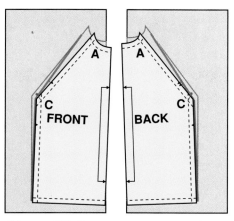

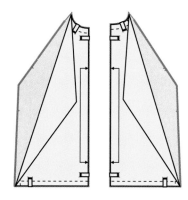

Diagram CC: Pivot to waist; trace side cutting line.

Diagram DD: Completed alteration to decrease bust on raglan-sleeve pattern

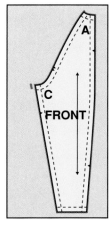
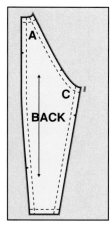

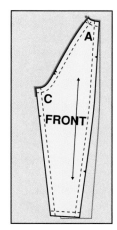
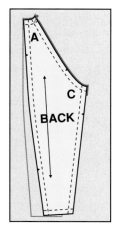

Diagram A: Outline sleeve pattern; mark increase.

Diagram B: Pivot to mark; trace raglan armhole cutting line.

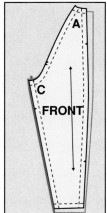
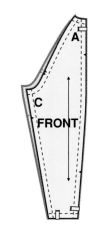

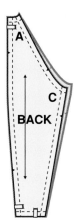

Diagram C: Pivot pattern to sleeve hem; trace underarm cutting line.

Diagram D: Completed alteration to increase two-piece raglan sleeve

DECREASING SLEEVE WIDTH

1. Outline the sleeve pattern on the work sheet. Measure in the needed decrease at the underarm, parallel to the side seam; mark (*Diagram A*).

2. Place a pin at pivot point A; pivot the pattern in to the decrease mark. Trace the raglan armhole and 1" of the side cutting line (*Diagram B*).

3. Keeping the pattern pivoted, move the pin to pivot point C; pivot the pattern to the hem outline. Trace the new underarm cutting line (*Diagram C*).

4. Repeat steps 1 through 3 on the other side of the raglan sleeve.

5. Match the pattern pieces to the original outlines; tape. Fold in the pattern sections that overlap the new outlines. Cut out, following the new outlines (*Diagram D*).

Note from Nancy: Diagrams A–D show the sleeve in the common two-piece version. On occasion, the raglan sleeve is one piece. Simply make changes on both sides of a one-piece raglan sleeve, using the same steps as for a two-piece sleeve (*Diagram E*).

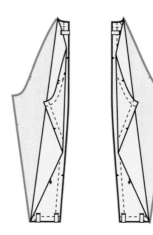

Raglan sleeves have diagonal seams from underarm to shoulder.

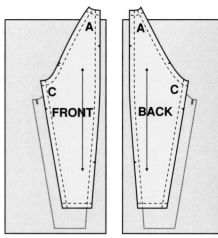

Diagram A: Outline each pattern piece; mark decrease.

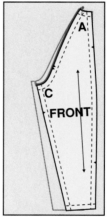

Diagram B: Pivot to mark; trace new armhole cutting line.

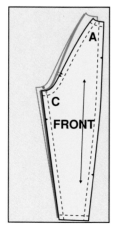

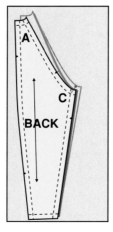

Diagram C: Pivot to hem; trace new underarm cutting line.

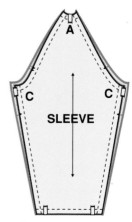

Diagram D: Completed alteration to decrease two-piece raglan sleeve

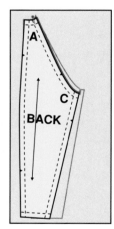

Diagram E: Completed alteration to increase one-piece raglan sleeve

Altering Tops with Yokes

A top with a yoke has horizontal seams across the upper back and just above the bust on the front. A decorative yoke uses two pattern pieces and has a shoulder seam. A one-piece yoke is made from a single piece of fabric that goes over both shoulders.

In a style with a yoke, even though the bodice is in two pieces, you can still make changes with Fitting Finesse. Use a separate work sheet for each pattern piece. Make sure the yoke work sheet is the same length and follows the same angles as the pattern and that it is wider than the yoke pattern.

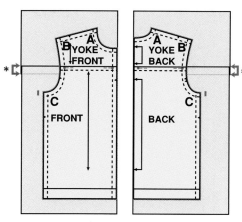

Diagram A: Overlap two work sheets by 1¼" (*). Pin pattern pieces together, stacking stitching lines. Outline pattern; mark increase.

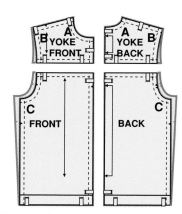

Diagram B: Completed alterations on separate work sheets for each pattern piece

ALTERING A TOP WITH A TWO-PIECE YOKE

1. Pin the front yoke pattern piece to the blouse front pattern piece, stacking stitching lines. Overlap the two work sheets by 1¼" (the total of both seam allowances); tape together.

2. Place the pattern on the work sheet, matching the stacked seam allowances to the overlapped work sheets. Outline the pattern (*Diagram A*).

3. Alter the front pattern piece as shown on page 24 for increasing the bust or page 25 for decreasing the bust.

4. Untape the work sheets and unpin the pattern pieces. Place the corresponding pattern pieces and work sheets together, matching the patterns to the original outline. Cut out, following the new outline.

5. Repeat steps 1 through 4 on the back pattern pieces (*Diagram B*).

Yokes can be one piece or have shoulder seams.

Altering A Top with a One-Piece Yoke

1. Pin the pattern pieces together, outline, and mark.

• Pin the yoke pattern piece to the blouse front pattern piece, stacking stitching lines.

• Lap the yoke work sheet over the front work sheet 1¼" (the total of both seam allowances); tape.

• Place the pattern pieces on the work sheets, matching the stacked seam allowances to the overlapped work sheets.

• Outline the pattern on the work sheet. Measure out the needed increase at the underarm area; mark (*Diagram A*). Measure in if decreasing.

2. Place a pin at pivot point B on the yoke pattern; pivot the pattern out to the increase mark. Pivot in, if decreasing. Trace the new armhole cutting line (*Diagram B*).

3. Keeping the pattern pivoted, move the pin to pivot point C; pivot in to the waist. Trace the new side cutting line (*Diagram C*).

4. Untape the work sheets and unpin the pattern pieces. Tape the pattern pieces to the original outlines on the work sheets. Cut out, following the new outlines.

5. Repeat steps 1 through 4 on the back pattern pieces, overlapping the opposite end of the yoke work sheet on the blouse back work sheet (*Diagram D*).

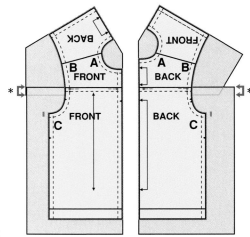

Diagram A: Pin work sheets together, overlapping 1¼" (*). Pin pattern pieces together, stacking stitching lines. Mark.

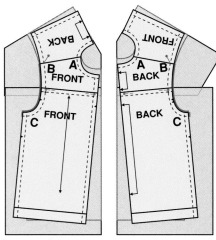

Diagram B: Pivot to mark; trace new armhole cutting line.

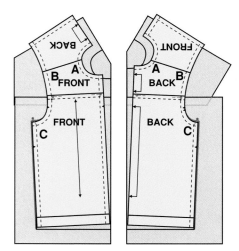

Diagram C: Pivot to waist; trace side cutting line.

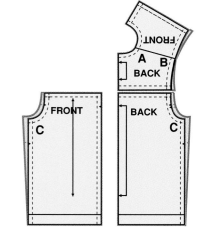

Diagram D: Completed alteration to increase bust on separate work sheet for each pattern piece

Altering Princess-Style Patterns

A princess-style garment's vertical seams make it extremely flattering, especially on full-busted women. A princess-style pattern has four main pieces: the center front, the side front, the center back, and the side back. This provides multiple seams where you can add many inches evenly without changing the style (and without using extensions).

Princess-style garments have six seams you can alter, giving you a total of 12 edges over which to spread changes. Your pattern may have a center back seam, but altering at this seam or at the center front fold throws off the grain line of your fabric. A small change at each side seam makes a significant change in the overall garment. For example, to add 6" at the bust, only add ½" at each seam. By the same token, waist and hip increases are divided by 12.

Preparing the Pattern

Draw the underarm line and mark pivot point BB on each pattern piece.

• Pin the center back to the side back pattern piece and the center front to the side front pattern piece at the underarm, stacking the stitching lines. Draw the underarm reference line as indicated on page 54.

• Add pivot points BB where the princess seams cross the shoulder seams on all four pieces (*Diagram*).

• Unpin the pattern pieces.

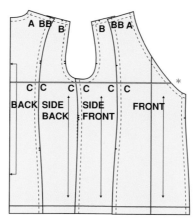

Diagram: Pin jacket pattern pieces together at underarm, stacking stitching lines. Draw underarm line (*); mark pivot point BB.

Princess styles have six seams (12 edges) over which you can spread changes.

Increasing the Bust and the Hip

In this section, both bust and hip alterations are shown simultaneously. It's a common combination of changes.

1. Outline the pattern on work sheets. Measure the needed bust increase from each side edge at the underarm line and the hip increase at the hip line; mark (*Diagrams A and B*).

2. Increase the underarm seams on the side front and side back pattern pieces.

• Place a pin at pivot point B; pivot the pattern to the underarm increase mark. Trace the new armhole cutting line (*Diagram C*).

• Keeping the pattern pivoted, move the pin to side seam pivot point C; pivot the pattern to the hip increase mark. Trace the new side cutting line between the underarm and hip (*Diagram D*). Return the pattern to its original position.

3. Increase the princess-style seams on the side front and side back pattern pieces.

• Place a pin at pivot point BB; pivot the pattern out to the underarm line increase mark. Trace between the shoulder and the underarm line (*Diagram E*).

• Keeping the pattern pivoted, move the pin to princess seam pivot point C; pivot the pattern to the increase mark at the hip. Trace the cutting line between the underarm line and the hip (*Diagram F*).

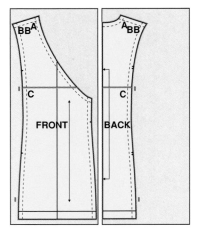

Diagram A: Outline pattern; mark increase at underarm and hip of jacket front and back pattern pieces.

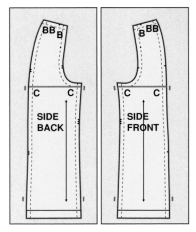

Diagram B: Outline; mark increase at underarm and hip of front and back side pattern pieces.

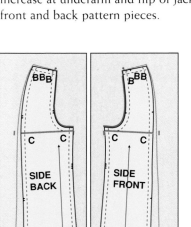

Diagram C: Pivot side to underarm mark; trace new armhole cutting line.

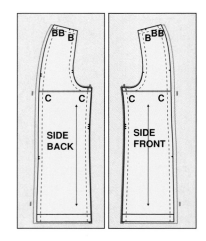

Diagram D: Pivot to hip mark; trace new side cutting line.

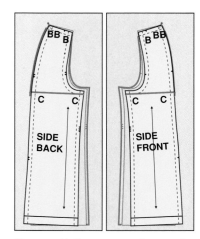

Diagram E: Pivot to mark at underarm line; trace from shoulder to underarm line.

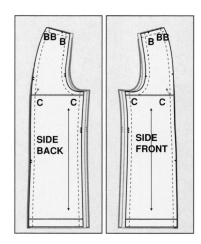

Diagram F: Pivot to hip mark; trace new side cutting line.

• Match the pattern pieces to the original outlines; tape. Cut out, following the new outline (*Diagram G*).

4. Alter the center front and center back pattern pieces.

• To increase the inner seam, place a pin at pivot point BB; pivot the pattern to the increase mark at the underarm line. Trace between the shoulder and the underarm line (*Diagram H*).

• Keeping the pattern pivoted, move the pin to princess seam pivot point C; pivot the pattern to the hip increase mark. Trace the side cutting line between the underarm line and the hip (*Diagram I*).

Note from Nancy: The illustrations show alterations on a jacket. To alter a princess-style dress, mark the same increase or decrease at the hem that you mark at the hip and pivot from the hip change (pivot point E) to the hem change. This preserves the hem width and the shape the dress designer intended.

5. Match the pattern pieces to the original outlines; tape. Cut out, following the new outlines (*Diagram J*).

Note from Nancy: There are two types of princess-style designs. The one for which I've given detailed fitting instructions has seams that lead into the shoulder. The other style is a curved princess style, where seams lead into the armhole. Both styles are altered in the same way, except that pivot point BB moves to a spot midway on the armhole for the curved princess style. The alterations for the curved princess style are made at the underarm line and the hipline (*Diagram K*).

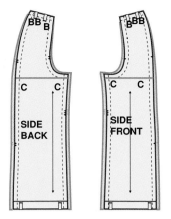

Diagram G: Completed alteration to increase bust and hip on jacket side front and side back pattern pieces

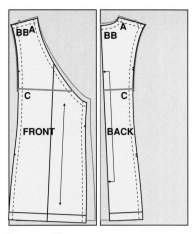

Diagram H: Pivot to underarm mark; trace from shoulder to underarm line.

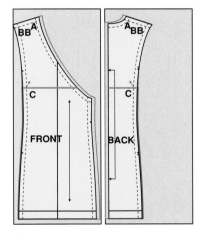

Diagram I: Pivot to hip mark; trace to hip.

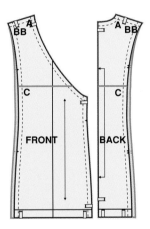

Diagram J: Completed alterations to increase bust and hip on center front and back jacket pattern pieces

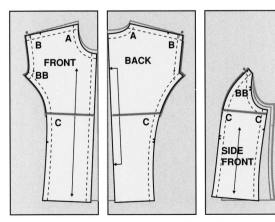

Diagram K: Pivot; trace pattern with princess seams going into armhole.

DECREASING

1. Outline the side front and side back pattern pieces on a work sheet. Measure the needed bust decrease from each side edge at the underarm line and the hip decrease at the hip line; mark (*Diagram A*).

2. Alter the underarm side seams.

• Place a pin at pivot point B; pivot the pattern in to the underarm decrease mark. Trace the new armhole cutting line (*Diagram B*).

• Keeping the pattern pivoted, move the pin to underarm pivot point C; pivot the pattern in to the hip decrease mark. Trace the new side cutting line between the underarm and the hip (*Diagram C*). Return the pattern to its original position.

3. Alter the princess-style seams.

• Place a pin at pivot point BB; pivot the pattern in to the underarm line decrease mark. Trace between the shoulder and the underarm line (*Diagram D*).

• Keeping the pattern pivoted, move the pin to princess seam pivot point C; pivot the pattern in to the decrease mark at the hip. Trace the side cutting line between the underarm line and the hip (*Diagram E*).

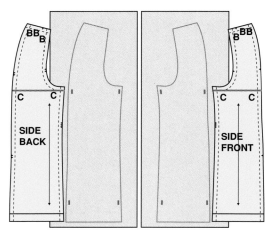

Diagram A: Outline; mark decrease at underarm and hip on each side.

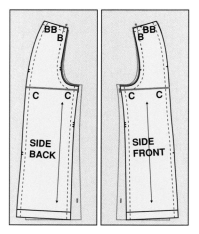

Diagram B: Pivot to underarm decrease mark; trace new armhole cutting lines.

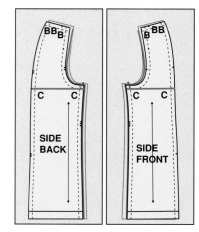

Diagram C: Pivot to hip mark; trace new side cutting line.

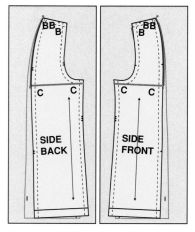

Diagram D: Pivot to underarm mark on other side; trace from shoulder to underarm line.

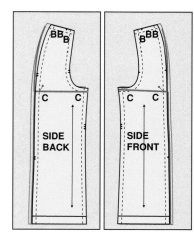

Diagram E: Pivot to hip mark; trace between underarm line and hip.

• Match the pattern to the original outlines; tape it to the work sheet. Fold in the pattern sections that overlap the new outline. Cut out, following the new outline (*Diagram F*).

4. Alter the center front and center back pattern pieces.

• Outline the center front and center back pattern pieces on a work sheet. Measure the needed bust decrease from each side edge at the underarm line and the hip decrease at the hip line; mark (*Diagram G*).

• To decrease the inner seam, place a pin at pivot point BB; pivot the pattern to the underarm mark. Trace between the shoulder and the underarm line (*Diagram H*).

• Keeping the pattern pivoted, move the pin to princess seam pivot point C; pivot the pattern to the hip mark. Trace the side cutting line between the underarm line and the hip (*Diagram I*).

5. Match the pattern pieces to the original outlines; tape. Cut out, following the new outlines (*Diagram J*).

Note from Nancy: These instructions show you how to alter in a single process both the hip and the bust on a princess-style dress. It's even easier to change only one of these areas.

To increase or decrease the bust (but not the hip), pivot from pivot point C to the original hip stitching line rather than to a hip mark. Do the same on the center front and center back pattern pieces in Step 4.

To alter the hip only, do not pivot from pivot point BB. Start instead with the pattern in its original, unaltered position and pivot from underarm pivot point C to the hip mark. When altering a dress, remember to pivot from the hip to the mark at the hem so that your garment keeps the overall lines the designer intended.

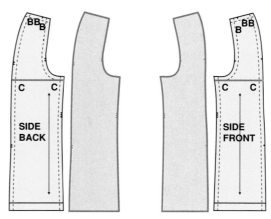

Diagram F: Completed alterations to decrease bust and hip on jacket side front and side back pattern pieces

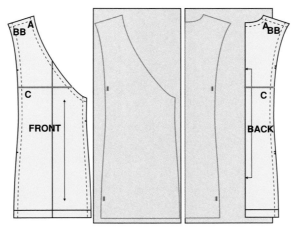

Diagram G: Outline; mark decrease at underarm and hip.

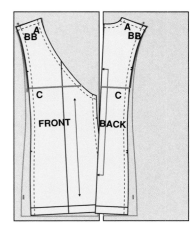

Diagram H: Pivot to underarm mark; trace from shoulder to underarm cutting line.

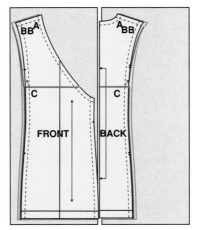

Diagram I: Pivot to hip mark; trace to hem.

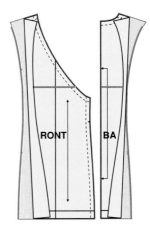

Diagram J: Completed alterations to jacket center front and center back pattern pieces

Combining Alterations on One Work Sheet

Up to this point, we have focused primarily on individual pattern alterations. Since most of us may need two or more changes on our patterns, it's important to learn how to combine changes.

The one work sheet approach allows you to make two or more alterations on the same work sheet. This is the express way to fitting, but to keep your changes accurate, you must follow a specific order for making alterations.

FRONT/BACK ALTERATIONS ORDER

1. Hem
2. Center (front or back)
3. Neckline
4. Shoulder
5. Armhole/Back width
6. Bust
7. Waist
8. Hip

Note from Nancy: Looking at the illustrations (*Diagram A*), notice that on the front piece you work counterclockwise and on the back piece you work clockwise.

SLEEVE ALTERATIONS ORDER

The order is slightly different when altering sleeves, since these have no center front or back. This is the sequence for altering the sleeves (*Diagram B*).

1. Hem
2. Cap
3. Side seams

If you need a sleeve to be both longer and wider, you first make the length change and then increase the sleeve's width.

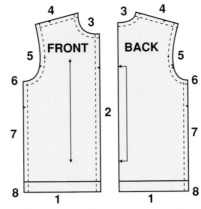

Diagram A: Alteration order for front and back pattern pieces

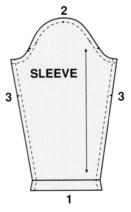

Diagram B: Alteration order for sleeve patterns

Pivot-and-slide techniques make it easy to combine alterations for perfect fit.

MAKING TYPICAL COMBINED ALTERATIONS

To help you see what order you should use, let's look at some typical alterations. I will use general directions for the examples. Consult the appropriate chapter for detailed instructions on making any of these individual alterations.

ALTERING THE SHOULDER AND THE BUST

Altering for square shoulders and increasing the bust is a typical combined alteration. I have abbreviated these directions. If you need more detailed instructions, refer to the appropriate chapters for individual alterations.

1. Outline the front pattern piece on the work sheet. Measure the needed changes for both alterations; mark the work sheet (*Diagram A*).

2. Pivot and trace the new shoulder cutting line.

• Work counterclockwise on the front pattern piece, starting with the square shoulder alteration. Work clockwise on the back pattern piece.

• Insert a pin at pivot point A; pivot the pattern to the square shoulder mark above the end of the shoulder seam. Trace the new shoulder cutting line (*Diagram B*).

3. Keeping the pattern pivoted, move the pin to pivot point B; pivot the pattern to the bust increase mark. Trace the new armhole cutting line (*Diagram C*).

4. Keeping the pattern pivoted, move the pin to pivot point C; pivot the pattern to the original waist outline. Trace the cutting line between the underarm and the waist (*Diagram D*).

5. Match the pattern pieces to the original outlines; tape. Cut out, following the new outlines (*Diagram E*).

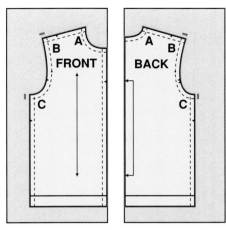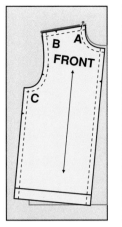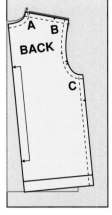

Diagram A: Outline; mark both alterations.

Diagram B: Pivot to shoulder mark; trace new shoulder.

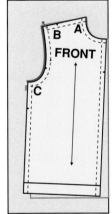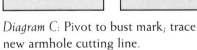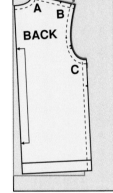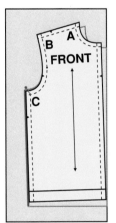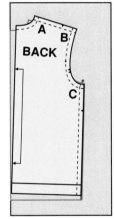

Diagram C: Pivot to bust mark; trace new armhole cutting line.

Diagram D: Pivot to waist; trace new side cutting lines.

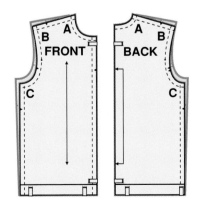

Diagram E: Completed bust and square shoulder alterations

INCREASING SLEEVE LENGTH AND WIDTH

1. Outline the pattern, extend the grain line, and mark.

• Outline only the hem area of the sleeve pattern on the work sheet. Extend the grain line.

• Measure up the needed hem increase from the bottom; mark (*Diagram A*).

• Slide the pattern up, following the grain line to the increase mark. Trace the rest of the pattern.

• Measure out the needed increase on each side of the underarm; mark (*Diagram B*).

2. Place a pin at sleeve pivot point B; pivot to the increase mark at one of the side seams. Trace half the cap and 1" around the corner of the sleeve (*Diagram C*).

3. Pivot and trace the side cutting line.

• Keeping the pattern pivoted, move the pin to pivot point C; pivot the pattern to the side cutting line near the hem. Trace the new side cutting line (*Diagram D*).

• Move the pattern to its original position in Step 2.

4. Repeat steps 3 and 4 on the other half of the sleeve.

5. Tape the pattern to the work sheet, matching the cap areas. Fold back the pattern at the hem area. Cut out, following the new outline (*Diagram E*).

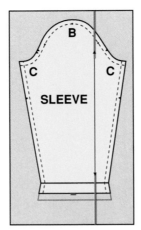

Diagram A: Outline hem; extend grain line. Measure increase up from hem; mark.

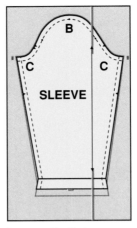

Diagram B: Slide pattern to mark; trace. Mark increase on each side of underarm.

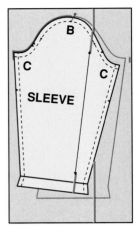

Diagram C: Pivot; trace half of sleeve cap cutting line.

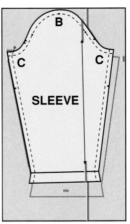

Diagram D: Pivot to hem; trace side cutting line.

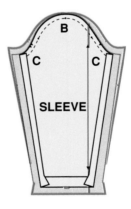

Diagram E: Completed alterations for longer and wider sleeve

ALTERING BACK, BUST, AND HIP

I have abbreviated these directions for lengthening the back, increasing the bust, and increasing the hip on a three-piece jacket. If you need more detailed instructions, refer to the appropriate individual alterations.

1. Outline the front and back pattern pieces. Measure the length needed on the back piece; mark. Measure out the needed increase at the bust and hip; mark (*Diagram A*).

2. Lengthen the back.

• Slide the back pattern piece up to the mark above the neckline. Trace the neck cutting line.

• Place a pin at pivot point A; pivot to the original outline at the armhole. Trace the shoulder cutting line (*Diagram B*).

3. Alter the front and back pattern pieces following instructions for individual alterations to increase the bust and the hip. Pivot the pattern twice (at pivot points B and C). Trace the new cutting lines (*Diagrams C and D*).

4. Match each pattern piece to its original outline; tape. Cut out, following the new outline. Measure the distance between the original outline and the alteration on each pattern at the armhole side seam; record on the patterns (*Diagram E*).

5. Alter the side panel.

• Outline the pattern. Extend the grain line. Measure up from the underarm cutting line the increase measured in Step 4; mark.

• Slide the pattern up. Trace the new armhole and 1″ of each side cutting line (*Diagram F*).

• Match the pattern to the original outline; tape. Cut out, following the new outline (*Diagram G*).

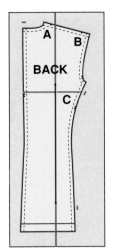 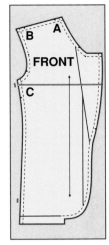 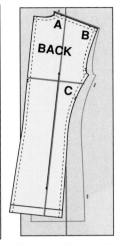 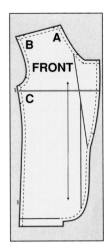

Diagram A: Outline pattern; mark increases.

Diagram B: Pivot back pattern piece; trace.

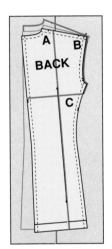 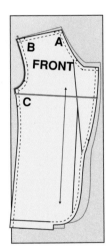 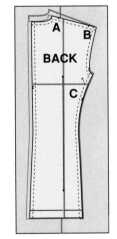 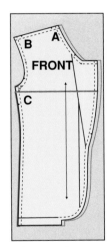

Diagram C: Pivot to mark at underarm; trace.

Diagram D: Pivot to hipline mark; trace.

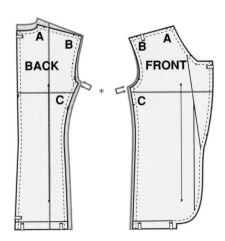 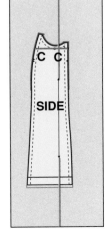 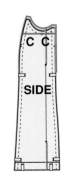

Diagram E: Cut out front and back pattern pieces; measure change (*).

Diagram F: Slide pattern up; trace.

Diagram G: Completed alterations on jacket side panel

Fitting Skirts with *Finesse*

Skirts are the easiest of all garments to fit, and pivot-and-slide techniques make the process even simpler. Whereas dresses and pants have a variety of curves and seams that may require adjustments, classic-style skirts have long, relatively straight seams. They only need altering for waist, hip, or length changes.

Using two key measurements—the waist and the hip—and the streamlined Fitting Finesse process, you'll be on your way to a perfectly fitted skirt!

Quick Reference

PATTERN SIZING

Purchase your skirt pattern by either the waist or hip measurement. If you fall between sizes, take your choice!

If the pattern includes several garment components (jacket, blouse, skirt, and pants), purchase the size according to your front width measurement (see page 9), since fitting a garment above the waist requires specific sizing.

Classic-style skirt

PIVOT POINTS

Skirt patterns have pivot points similar to those on dress patterns. On the front and the back of a skirt pattern, mark the following three basic pivot points:

D—Point where the waist and side seam stitching lines cross

E—Point where the hip line and side seam stitching line cross

F—Point where the center front/back intersects the waist stitching line

DRAWING REFERENCE LINES

When instructions call for extending the grain line or adding a reference line (hipline), use a yardstick and a marking pen to draw on the pattern piece. Transfer the line to the work sheet by using a tracing wheel. Place the pattern on top of the work sheet; trace along the line. The tracing wheel points will perforate the work sheet, producing a guideline.

Grain Lines

Extend the grain line the full length of the pattern and the work sheet to make it easier to slide the pattern up and down when changing length.

Hip Line

For a hip line, measure down from the waistline on the pattern piece the amount of your hipline length (see page 11 for how to take this measurement). Draw this reference line directly on the skirt front and back pattern pieces.

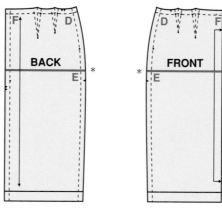

Skirt pivot points with hip line marked (*)

Fast Waist Changes

An easy slide and pivot of the pattern can quickly add or subtract inches from the pattern waistline. Make these changes at the side seams to maintain the grain line and the style of the pattern.

Determining Changes

Compare your waist measurement on the Personal Fitting Chart (page 141) to the measurement on the back of the pattern envelope. For example:

Actual measurement	27"
Pattern envelope	25"
Alteration	+2"

Divide the alteration amount by four, the number of cut edges at both side seams. In the example, ½" would be added to each cut edge.

INCREASING

1. Outline the pattern and mark the increase.

- Outline the front pattern piece on a work sheet.
- Measure out from the waist for the increase; mark (*Diagram A*).

2. Slide the pattern to the mark; trace the wider waist.

3. Place a pin at pivot point D; pivot the pattern in to the original outline at the hip. Trace the new cutting line between the waist and the hip (*Diagram B*).

4. Match the pattern to the original outline; tape. Cut out, following the new outline.

5. Repeat steps 1 through 4 on the back pattern piece (*Diagram C*). Alter the waistband if necessary. (See "Altering the Waistband," page 76.)

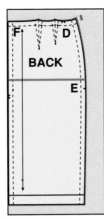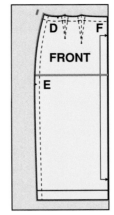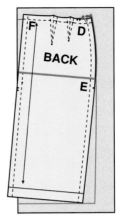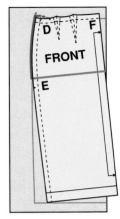

Diagram A: Outline pattern; mark increase.

Diagram B: Slide to mark at waist. Pivot pattern to outline at hip; trace.

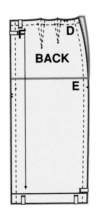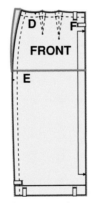

Diagram C: Completed alterations for larger waist

DECREASING

1. Outline the front pattern piece on a work sheet. Measure in at the waist for the decrease amount; mark (*Diagram A*).
2. Slide the pattern to the mark.
3. Place a pin at pivot point D; pivot the pattern out to the original outline at the hip. Trace the new cutting line between the waist and the hip (*Diagram B*).
4. Match the pattern to the original outline; tape. Fold in the pattern sections that overlap the new outline. Cut out, following the new outline.
5. Repeat steps 1 through 4 on the back pattern piece (*Diagram C*). Alter the waistband if necessary.

ALTERING THE WAISTBAND

Changing a waistband is the simplest of all altering techniques, but transferring the markings has been another story—until now.

INCREASING

1. Outline the waistband pattern piece on a work sheet; mark the increase to correspond to the amount added to the skirt waist.
2. Slide the pattern to the mark; trace the new cutting lines. Cut out, following the new outline (*Diagram AA*).
3. Place a length of elastic longer than the original waistband pattern piece along the notched lengthwise edge of the pattern. Match one end of the elastic to one pattern end; mark the opposite pattern end on the elastic.
4. Transfer pattern markings (single and double notches, center front, circles, and squares) to the elastic with a marking pen (*Diagram BB*).

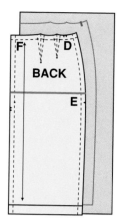 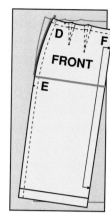

Diagram A: Outline pattern; mark decrease.

Diagram B: Slide to mark. Pivot pattern to outline at hip; trace new cutting line from waist to hip.

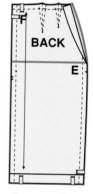 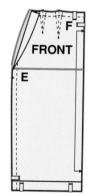

Diagram C: Completed alterations for smaller waist

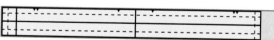

Diagram AA: Cut out enlarged waistband pattern piece.

Diagram BB: Mark pattern ends on elastic; transfer pattern markings to elastic.

Note from Nancy: It's not necessary to cut the elastic to a particular size as long as it's longer than your waistband. Since you only need it for the markings, use a length from your sewing basket. When you're done, you can still use it for sewing.

5. Stretch the elastic so that the pattern end markings match the work sheet; secure the elastic to the work sheet. Transfer the markings to the work sheet. This proportionally increases the pattern markings to fit the altered waistband (*Diagram CC*).

Note from Nancy: It helps to have three hands to carry out this quick alteration! If your sewing buddy isn't available, pin both the pattern and the elastic to the carpet to anchor the stretched elastic while you transfer the markings.

DECREASING

Elastic is the key to marking a smaller waistband as well. Just reverse the order of the steps you used to mark an increased waistband.

1. Outline the waistband pattern piece on a work sheet. Mark the decrease to correspond to the amount subtracted from the waist.

2. Slide pattern to the mark; trace the new cutting lines. Cut out, following the new outline.

3. Fold back one end of the waistband pattern piece the amount decreased from the waistband. Place a length of elastic longer than the original waistband pattern piece along the notched edge of the work sheet. Mark the decreased size of the waistband on the elastic (*Diagram A*).

4. Unfold the pattern to its original size; match the end of the elastic to one end of the pattern. Stretch the elastic to the original pattern size; trace the pattern markings (single and double notches, center front, circles, and squares) onto the elastic with a marking pen (*Diagram B*).

5. Release the elastic, match the end markings to the work sheet, and secure it to the work sheet. Transfer the markings from the elastic to the work sheet (*Diagram C*).

Diagram CC: Stretch elastic to fit work sheet pattern; transfer markings to work sheet.

Skirt with fitted waistband

Diagram A: Fold pattern decrease amount; mark decreased size on elastic.

Diagram B: Stretch elastic to length of waistband pattern; transfer marks.

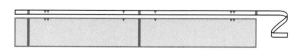

Diagram C: Relax elastic; transfer marks to work sheet.

ALTERING A SKIRT WITH SIDE POCKETS

1. Matching the dots and the notches, pin the lining pattern piece to the skirt front pattern piece, with the pocket pattern piece sandwiched in between the other pieces (*Diagrams A and B*).

2. Place two work sheets over the first work sheet in the pocket area; tape all three together (*Diagram C*).

3. Outline the pattern pieces on the work sheets with a tracing wheel so that the spokes of the tracing wheel perforate all three work sheet layers. Outline the back pattern piece with a marker (*Diagram D*).

4. Alter the front pattern piece according to the instructions on page 75 ("Increasing") or page 76 ("Decreasing"). Trace over the new cutting lines with a tracing wheel. Alter the back pattern piece; trace the new cutting lines with a marker (*Diagram E*).

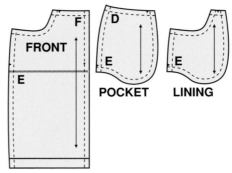
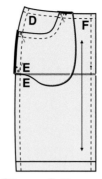

Diagram A: Pattern pieces for skirt with side pockets

Diagram B: Pin pocket and lining pattern pieces to front pattern piece.

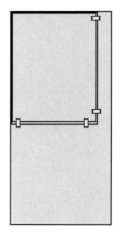
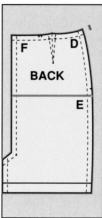
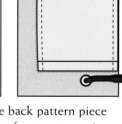

Diagram C: Tape pocket and lining work sheets to front work sheet.

Diagram D: Outline back pattern piece with marker; outline front pattern piece with tracing wheel. Mark increase.

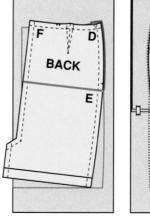
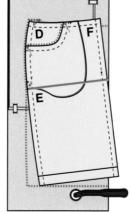

Diagram E: Alter pattern; trace new cutting lines.

5. Separate the pattern pieces, trace, and cut.

• Untape the pattern pieces and the work sheets. Place the respective pattern pieces and work sheets together, matching pattern pieces to original outlines; tape. Trace remaining sides of the lining and pocket pattern pieces (*Diagram F*).

• Cut out the pocket and lining pattern pieces, following the new outlines.

• Cut out the skirt front and back pattern pieces, following the new outlines (*Diagram G*).

• Alter the waistband by the same amount added to the skirt waist (see page 76).

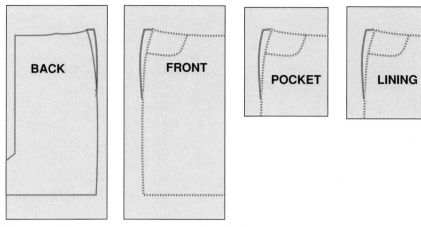

Diagram F: Untape pattern pieces and work sheets.

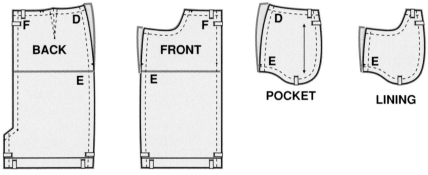

Diagram G: Completed alteration for larger waist on skirt, pocket, and lining pattern pieces

Skirt with side pockets

Hip Changes

Hip changes are among the most common alterations made. To maintain the style of the pattern, you'll be adding or subtracting the same amount at the hip and hem.

Determining Changes

Compare your hip measurement on the fitting chart (page 141) with the hip measurement for your size on the pattern back. The difference between the two equals the needed alteration. For example:

Actual measurement	40"
Pattern envelope	36"
Alteration	+4"

Divide the alteration by four, the number of cut edges. In the example, add 1" to each side of both the front and back pattern pieces.

INCREASING

1. Outline the pattern on a work sheet. Measure the needed increase out from both the hip cutting line and the bottom cutting line; mark (*Diagram A*).

2. Place a pin at pivot point D; pivot the pattern out to the increase mark at the hip. Trace the new cutting line between the waist and the hip (*Diagram B*).

3. Keeping the pattern pivoted, move the pin to pivot point E; pivot the pattern to the increase mark at the hem. Trace the new cutting line between the hip and the hem (*Diagram C*).

4. Match the pattern to the original outline; tape it to the work sheet. Cut out, following the new outline.

5. Repeat steps 1 through 4 on the back pattern piece (*Diagram D*).

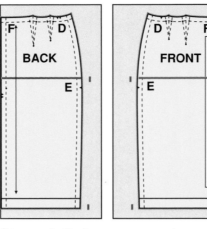
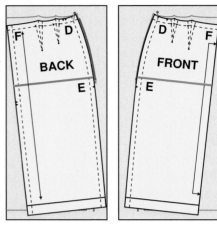

Diagram A: Outline pattern; mark increase at both hip and hem.

Diagram B: Pivot pattern to hip increase; trace new cutting line from waist to hip.

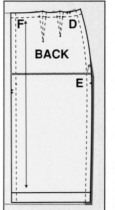
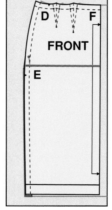
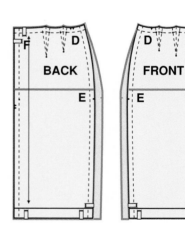

Diagram C: Pivot pattern to hem increase; trace new cutting line from hip to hem.

Diagram D: Completed alteration for larger hip

DECREASING

1. Outline the pattern on a work sheet. Measure the needed decrease in from both the hip cutting line and the bottom cutting line; mark (*Diagram A*).

2. Place a pin at pivot point D; pivot the pattern in to the decrease mark at the hip. Trace the new cutting line between the waist and the hip (*Diagram B*).

3. Keeping the pattern pivoted, move the pin to pivot point E; pivot the pattern to the decrease mark at the hem. Trace the new cutting line between the hip and the hem (*Diagram C*).

4. Match the pattern to the original outline; tape it to the work sheet. Fold in the pattern sections that overlap the new outline. Cut out, following the new outline.

5. Repeat steps 1 through 4 on the back pattern piece (*Diagram D*).

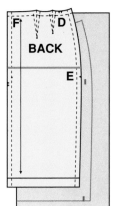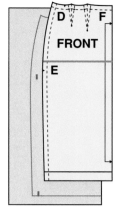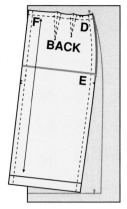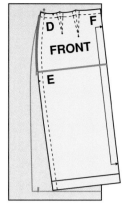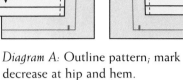

Diagram A: Outline pattern; mark decrease at hip and hem.

Diagram B: Pivot pattern to hip mark; trace new cutting line from waist to hip.

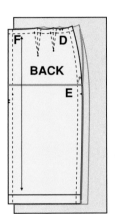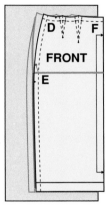

Diagram C: Pivot pattern to hem mark; trace new cutting line from hip to hem.

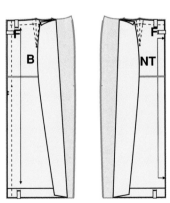

Diagram D: Completed alteration for smaller hip

Add or subtract inches from hip with Fitting Finesse.

FITTING FOR A HIGH HIP

If you have one hip that is slightly higher than the other, the fabric of your skirts pulls with diagonal stress wrinkles on the higher side, resulting in an uneven hem. If you have a high hip, avoid plaids and stripes, which accentuate the changes made to fit the garment.

Note from Nancy: It is fairly common to have one high hip on the side opposite one square shoulder. See "Square Shoulders" on page 39.

1. Outline the front pattern piece on the work sheet.

2. Use a fashion ruler to add shape between the waist and the hip, creating a more predominant curve; redraw the side seam cutting line *(Diagram A)*.

3. Alter the back pattern piece following the same steps.

4. Match the pattern to the original outline; tape. Cut out the pattern, following the new outline. Cut out the skirt. Untape the pattern from the work sheet.

Note from Nancy: The alteration in Step 2 affects both side seams. I find it easier and faster to cut both sides of a skirt with the high hip alteration; then trim the excess fabric from the lower hip side.

5. Trim the excess fabric from the lower hip side.

• On the *right* (not wrong) side of your fabric, mark the side of the pattern that corresponds to your high hip (right or left).

• Place the pattern on the side of the skirt that does *not* accommodate the high hip. Double-check to be sure you cut the correct side.

• Trim the excess fabric from the lower hip side on both the front and back pattern pieces *(Diagram B)*.

• Alter the waistband by the same amount as the skirt waist.

High hip causes stress wrinkles on one side of skirt.

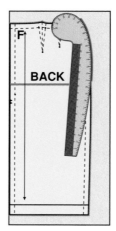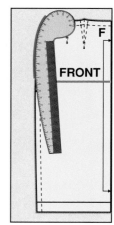

Diagram A: Use fashion ruler to add shape between waist and hip on high hip side.

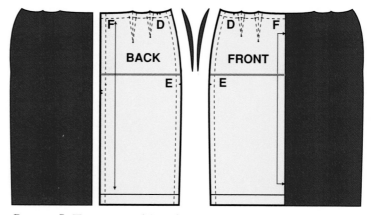

Diagram B: Trim excess fabric from lower hip side.

Note from Nancy: "High hip" most often refers to having one side higher than the other. But if your figure is full above both hips and below the waist, this is also called "high hip." To fit a skirt with both high hips, follow steps 1 through 4 for "Fitting for a High Hip." This provides the alteration you need for both sides.

Hem Changes

The slide technique is used to add or subtract length to a skirt pattern. Extend the grain line (see page 74) and use this as a guideline when sliding your pattern up or down.

Note from Nancy: The advantages of changing the skirt length by sliding the pattern are that it keeps the pattern intact and the shape at the side seams remains even. It may seem faster and easier just to cut the pattern longer or shorter, but generally that super-quick method is not as accurate.

Determining Changes

Compare the pattern length to your figure.

• Pin the natural waist of the front pattern to the waist of your undergarment. Align the center front of the pattern with your undergarment's center front; pin (*Diagram A*).

• Walk the skirt pattern piece down your figure, pinch the pattern at the desired length, and mark it with a pencil (*Diagram B*). Unpin the pattern.

• Using the hem allowance from the pattern, draw the hemline parallel to the bottom cutting line. Measure from your hemline to the pattern's hemline. This is the amount to lengthen or to shorten the skirt.

Diagram B: Pinch pattern at desired length.

Diagram A: Meet pattern center front to figure center front; pin.

Sliding changes skirt length but not shape.

LENGTHENING

1. Outline the pattern and mark the increase.

• On a work sheet, outline only the bottom cutting line and 1" along the side seam and center front of the skirt front pattern piece.

• Measure the needed alteration up from the bottom cutting line; mark (*Diagram A*).

2. Slide the pattern up to the mark, following the grain line.

3. Trace the rest of the side cutting line, the waist, and the center front (*Diagram B*).

4. Without moving the pattern, tape it to the work sheet. Cut out, following the new outline.

5. Repeat steps 1 through 4 on the back pattern piece (*Diagram C*).

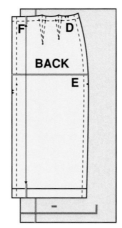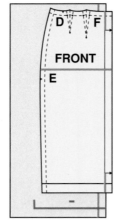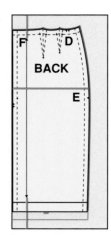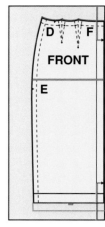

Diagram A: Outline hem cutting line and 1" of side seams and center front. Mark increase.

Diagram B: Slide pattern up to mark; trace.

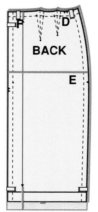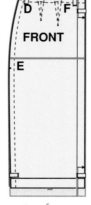

Diagram C: Completed alteration for longer straight skirt

Side seams of straight skirt stay true when lengthened by sliding.

SHORTENING

1. Outline the pattern and mark the decrease.

• On a work sheet, outline only the bottom cutting line and 1" along the side seam and the center front of the front pattern piece.

• Measure down from the bottom cutting line the amount needed to shorten the pattern; mark (*Diagram A*).

2. Slide the pattern down to the mark, following the grain line.

3. Trace the rest of the side cutting line, the waist, and the center front (*Diagram B*).

4. Without moving the pattern, tape it to the work sheet. Fold in the pattern sections that overlap the new outline. Cut out, following the new outline.

5. Repeat steps 1 through 4 on the back pattern piece (*Diagram C*).

Note from Nancy: On a gore, flared, or A-line skirt, taper the side seam to meet the width outlined at the hem. This step will keep the hem the same width as the pattern designer intended (*Diagrams D and E*).

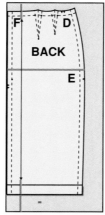
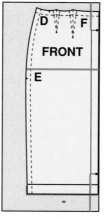
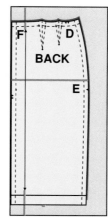
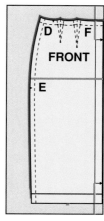

Diagram A: Outline hem cutting line and 1" of side seam; mark decrease.

Diagram B: Slide down to mark; trace.

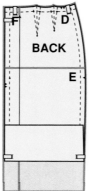
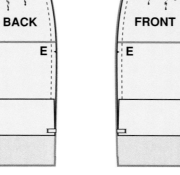
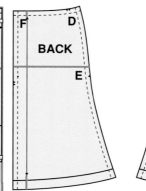
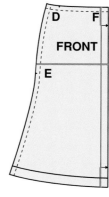

Diagram C: Completed alteration for shortening a straight skirt

Diagram D: Front and back pattern pieces for a gore skirt

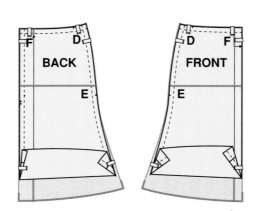

Diagram E: Taper side seam to maintain skirt's original hem width on completed alterations to shorten gore skirt.

Gore skirt

Combining Alterations

Sometimes you need more than one alteration on a skirt to achieve Fitting Finesse. You have two options: Make each alteration on a separate work sheet and then tape them together, or take a streamlined approach and do all changes on one work sheet.

Here's the easy one work sheet approach. For accuracy, work around the pattern in a circular sequence: clockwise for the back pattern piece and counterclockwise for the front pattern piece. The sequence naturally flows around the pattern, keeping the pattern's grain line on target. Follow the sequence listed below when combining alterations on a skirt (*Diagram*).

ONE WORK SHEET APPROACH

1. Hem—Hem changes should be the first priority with a one work sheet approach. Outline the hem, and then slide up or down to shorten or to lengthen the pattern. After changing the length, outline the remaining cutting lines and mark all the needed changes on the work sheet.

2. Center—If you have a sway-back alteration, make that change next on the skirt pattern.

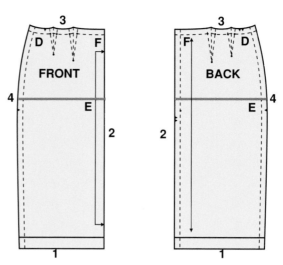

Diagram: Work clockwise around back pattern piece and counterclockwise on front pattern piece when combining alterations on one work sheet.

Note from Nancy: A swayback cannot be measured; it's only visible during the fine-tuning stage of fitting (page 122). If you find and correct for a swayback, on future skirt projects you can incorporate the change as needed when you make other alterations.

3. Waist—The third sequence is the waist area. If you need to increase or decrease the waist or to alter for a high hip, make these changes next.

4. Hip—The last area to alter when combining changes on one work sheet is the hip area.

Fitting Finesse works as easily for multiple alterations as for one.

LONGER SKIRT AND INCREASED WAIST AND HIP

1. Outline the pattern and mark the hem change.

• Outline only the bottom cutting line of the front pattern and 1" along the side seam and the center front on a work sheet.

• Measure the needed alteration up from the bottom cutting line; mark (*Diagram A*). If shortening the pattern, measure down.

2. Slide the pattern up to the mark, following the grain line. Trace the waist and the side cutting lines on the work sheet (*Diagram B*).

3. Make increases at both the hip and the waist.

• Measure the waist increase amount out; mark.

• Measure the hip increase amount out at both the hip and the hem; mark (*Diagram C*).

• Slide the pattern to the waist increase mark. Trace the waist.

• Place a pin at pivot point D; pivot the pattern to the hip increase mark. Trace the new cutting line between the waist and the hip (*Diagram D*).

4. Keeping the pattern pivoted, move the pin to pivot point E; pivot to the mark at the hem. Trace the new cutting line between the hip and the hem (*Diagram E*).

5. Match the pattern to the original outline; tape. Cut out, following the new outline. Repeat steps 1 through 4 on the back pattern piece (*Diagram F*).

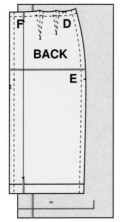
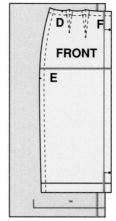

Diagram A: Outline hem cutting line and 1". Mark increase above hemline.

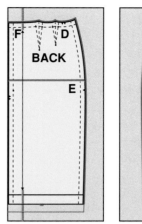

Diagram B: Slide pattern up to mark; trace waist and side cutting lines.

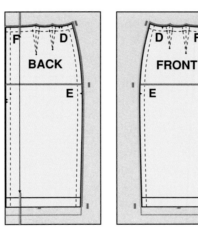

Diagram C: Mark increases at waist, hip, and hem.

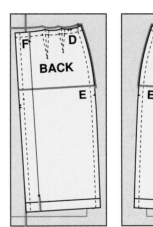

Diagram D: Slide to waist increase; trace. Pivot to hip increase; trace from waist to hip.

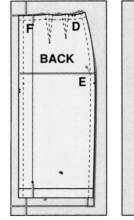
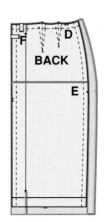

Diagram E: Pivot to hem increase; trace side cutting line from hip to hem.

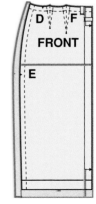

Diagram F: Completed alterations for longer skirt with wider hip and waist

Pants Fitting Finesse

Through my years of teaching sewing skills at seminars and on television, I have found that programs on fitting pants have always been popular. Why? Because fitting pants can be a challenge. Luckily, that challenge is easily met by using a specific plan for fitting.

The pant fitting plan has four basic steps: choose the correct size, measure your figure, measure the pattern pieces, and alter the pattern. You'll be rewarded with a great-looking, comfortable pair of pants.

Choosing the Right Size

The traditional guideline for pants has been to buy the pattern according to your hip measurement. However, when this measurement is used to choose a size, too often the hip of the pants may fit properly, but the legs bag like pajamas, and the crotch hangs too low.

An easy solution is to choose a smaller pattern size and alter it to fit the hip. Remember: It is much easier to enlarge a pattern than to reduce it. A smaller pattern size keeps the legs tapered and the crotch proportional.

MEASURING TO DETERMINE SIZE

To fit pant patterns the Fitting Finesse way, choose a pattern according to the Pant Pattern Size Chart. Most likely, you'll buy a smaller pattern size than you have in the past and then alter it to enlarge the hip.

• Measure the fullest part of your hip, making sure that the tape measure is parallel with the floor (*Diagram*).

• Refer to the Fitting Finesse Pant Pattern Size Chart on this page or on page 139 to determine which size to purchase.

• Buy a classic-style pattern for pants with a fitted waistband.

Note from Nancy: The Fitting Finesse Pant Pattern Size Chart works well in two ways. Choosing the smaller size eliminates the baggy fit in the legs and the low-hanging crotch. Plus, fitting into a smaller size makes anyone feel good!

Additional Sizing Guidelines

• If your hip measurement falls between sizes and your thighs are proportional to your hip, choose the size closest to your hip measurement. If your thighs are slender compared

The hip fits but nothing else does.

Diagram: Measure fullest part of hip.

to your hip, choose the smaller size. Use the larger size if your thighs are heavier.

• If your hip measurement is greater than 50", use the Misses' size 22 pattern.

• If you prefer another pattern type (Half Size, for example), use the more detailed chart on page 139.

Note from Nancy: I never recommend using a pattern larger than a size 22, because larger pattern sizes create pant legs that are uncontrollably baggy. It's much easier to make the hip area larger than it is to make all other areas smaller.

FITTING FINESSE PANT PATTERN SIZE CHART

Hip Measurement	Misses' Size
34"	6
36"	8
38"	10
40"	12
42"	14
44"	16
46"	18
48"	20
50"+	22

Measuring Your Figure

The next step to fitting pants with finesse is to take six measurements of your figure. Three of these are length measurements—pant length, side curve, and crotch—and three are width measurements—waist, hip, and thigh. To achieve a great fit, you must measure and compare the first five of these with the pattern measurements, but the thigh measurement is only necessary if the widest part of your figure is in the thigh area. For convenience, record all of these measurements on your Personal Fitting Chart for Pants (page 139).

Note from Nancy: For best results, recruit your sewing buddy to help take these measurements. Work as a team so that you can both make pants that fit.

Pant Length

To make it easy to figure out where to stop and start measuring pant length, wear a pair of pants that are a comfortable length. Have your sewing buddy measure the side seam from your "shelf" (below the waist but above the hipbone, where your pants actually rest) to the finished length (Diagram A).

Side Curve Length

Most of us are concerned with the number of inches around our figure, but the hip's shape and curve are also extremely important. A high, curvy hip needs more side length than usual. A low, flat hip needs less.

Note from Nancy: If you've ever noticed that the crease on one pant leg hangs straight and the other bows out, it's caused by one hip being higher than the other—a very common figure trait!

Diagram A: Measure pant length from shelf to finished hem.

Diagram B: Long side curve (left) makes crease bow in; short side curve (right) makes crease bow out.

The side length affects the way creases hang. If the side seam is too long, creases hang inward. If it's too short, creases bow out (Diagram B).

The side curve length is measured from the shelf to the crotch line. To measure the side curve:
- Stitch an elastic strip in a circle and place it around your leg to show your crotch line (or wear a pair of brief-style panties and use the leg elastic on them).
- Slide your thumb down your side from the waist until it rests on your shelf.
- Measure to the closest ½" from your shelf to your pantie line.
- Repeat this procedure on the other side; record both measurements (Diagram C).

Note from Nancy: Measure both side curve lengths. If there is a difference, use the longer measurement.

Diagram C: Slide thumb down to find shelf; measure from there to pantie line.

Crotch Length

For most people, fitting the crotch presents the biggest challenge to making pants that fit well. If the crotch length is too short, wrinkles radiate from the seat area. If the length is too long, the crotch hangs too low. In either case, the pants are uncomfortable to wear.

Fitting the crotch with finesse is a two-step process, and you'll learn both steps in this chapter. The first step is to measure your figure using the instructions below. Then read on to determine where to make changes.

To measure the crotch length:

• Use the same shelf (above the hip but below the waist, where the waist seam of a comfortable pair of pants rests) that you used to measure the pant and side curve lengths. Those two measurements were taken from the side shelf, and the crotch length is taken from the same area below your waist at center front and back.

• Place one end of the tape measure at the front shelf and run the tape between your legs; stop at the back shelf (generally, the deepest part of the sway in your back). Take this measurement exactly the way you want your pants to fit, not too tight or too loose; record (*Diagram*).

Crotch length that's too short causes wrinkles under seat (left); too long causes wrinkles in front (right).

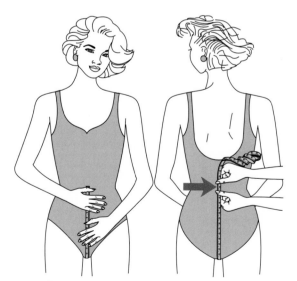

Diagram: Measure crotch from front shelf to back shelf.

Adding Ease

Pant patterns vary a great deal in their actual width measurements. One designer may allow more room in the seat than others, while another styles the pants wider in the thighs or the waist. Because of this variety, you'll need to compare your body width measurements to width measurements you take from the pant pattern.

Pattern widths always include ease (extra inches for comfort and style). As part of the Fitting Finesse method, you add a specific amount of ease to each body width measurement *before* recording it on the fitting chart for pants so that comparisons to pattern widths will be accurate.

Waist

• To take this measurement, first bend to the side; the deepest resulting wrinkle is your waist *(Diagram A)*. Stand straight again and measure around your waist, keeping the tape measure parallel to the floor. Place a thumb or a finger underneath the tape measure to prevent the measurement from being taken too tightly. Measure to the closest ½" *(Diagram B)*.

• Add 1" of ease to this measurement before recording it.

Hip

• Measure the fullest part of the hip, keeping the tape measure parallel to the floor and your finger underneath the tape to make sure it is not too tight *(Diagram C)*. Measure to the closest ½".

• Add 3" of ease to this measurement before recording it.

Thigh

It is only necessary to measure your thigh if the widest part of your figure is in the thigh area.

• Measure the fullest part of either upper leg *(Diagram D)*.

• Add 2" of ease to this measurement before recording it.

Diagram A: Bend to side; deepest wrinkle is waist.

Diagram B: Measure to closest ½".

Diagram C: Measure hip at fullest part.

Diagram D: Measure fullest part of either leg.

Preparing Pant Patterns

Fitting Finesse for pants relies on simple pivot-and-slide techniques for pattern alteration. This five-step process allows you to custom-fit clothes using work sheets made of inexpensive waxed paper or tissue paper. To pivot your pattern like a pendulum, insert a straight pin at a key point or slide the pattern along a straight grain line to make it larger or smaller. Your original pattern remains intact.

Detailed instructions for using pivot-and-slide techniques are given on page 18.

DRAWING REFERENCE LINES

When instructions call for adding a reference line or extending the grain line, use a yardstick and a marking pen to draw on the pattern.

Transfer the line to the work sheet by using a tracing wheel. Place the pattern on top of the work sheet; trace along the line. The tracing wheel points will perforate the work sheet, producing a guideline.

Grain Lines

Extend the grain line the full length of the pattern and the work sheet to make it easier to slide the pattern up and down when changing length (*Diagram A*).

Reference Lines

Reference lines should be drawn perpendicular to the grain line printed on the pattern.

For a crotch line, use the point where the crotch and inseam stitching lines intersect to position the line.

For a hip line, measure 2" above the crotch line.

For a knee line, locate the point midway between the crotch line and the hemline.

Note from Nancy: You've probably never been asked to find the knee line of a pattern before! Rest assured, you're not going to fit the pattern at the knee. You will only use that area as a pivot point. To find the knee line easily, fold the pattern up, meeting the hem to the crotch line. The fold will indicate the knee line.

PIVOT POINTS FOR PANTS

Mark the following pivot points on your patterns (*Diagram B*):

D—Point where the waist and the side seam stitching lines cross

E—Points where the hip line crosses the stitching line at the center seam and at the side seam

F—Point where the center and the waist stitching lines cross

G—Points where the crotch line crosses the stitching line at the inseam and at the side seam

H—Points where the knee line crosses the stitching line at the inseam and at the side seam.

READING DIAGRAMS

Remember that red lines in the illustrations indicate changes being made, and green lines represent changes completed in an earlier step.

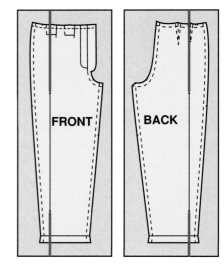

Diagram A: Extend grain line.

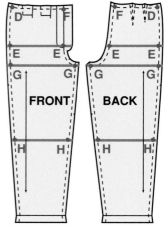

Diagram B: Pant pivot points

Measuring the Pattern

In earlier chapters, we used the ease allowed in the pattern and simply compared our measurements to the measurements written on the back of the pattern envelope. But with pants, my experience shows it is worth the extra step of comparing your measurements (including ease) to the actual pattern measurements. This more specific plan will give you greater Fitting Finesse! Record the pattern measurements and alteration amounts on the fitting chart for pants (page 139).

Note from Nancy: It's important to measure the pattern's side curve first and then, with the tape measure in the same place, check the pattern pant length. Both of these measurements are taken on the side and work in tandem to give you the best fit along the outer side seam.

Pattern Side Curve

• Use the front pattern piece for this measurement.

• Find your side curve measurement on the tape measure. Hold this point on the tape measure to the pattern at the crotch line along the side seam (*Diagram A*).

Note from Nancy: The crotch line should be printed on the front pattern piece. If not, simply draw a line perpendicular to the grain line from the crotch point to the side seam.

• If the tape measure ends below the waist stitching line, lay the other end of the tape measure so that the tab ends match. Read the amount shown on the tape at the stitching line; record (*Diagram B*).

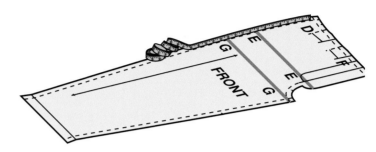

Diagram A: Measure side curve on pattern.

Diagram B: If tape measure ends below waist seam, lay other end of tape measure so that tab ends meet; read amount shown on tape at stitching line.

Diagram C: If tape measure extends above waist seam, read measurement at waist stitching line.

• If the tape measure extends above the waist stitching line, read the measurement at the waist stitching line; record (*Diagram C*).

Note from Nancy: Don't worry about additions or subtractions that are less than ¼". I always weigh more on Mondays than on Fridays, yet my clothes still fit!

Pattern Pant Length

- Keep the tape measure held to the crotch line at your side curve measurement.

- Add the hem allowance amount from the pattern to the pant length measurement from the fitting chart for pants to give you the cutting line of the hem. For example, if the pattern allows a 1½" hem, add 1½" to your pant length recorded on the chart.

- To measure the difference between the cutting line of the hem on the pattern and your measurement, lay the tape measure flat and extend it to the cutting line of the pattern piece (*Diagram A*).

- If the measurement for your cutting line is above the pattern cutting line, lay the other end of the tape measure so that the tab end meets the amount for your cutting line. Read the measurement at the cutting line; record (*Diagram B*).

- If the measurement for your cutting line is below the pattern cutting line, lay the other end of the tape measure so that the tab end meets the pattern cutting line. Read the measurement at the marked length; record (*Diagram C*).

Pattern Crotch Length

- Pin the crotch points together, stacking stitching lines.

- Place the end of the tape measure at the center back waist stitching line. Stand the tape measure on edge and place it around the curved stitching line to the center front waist stitching line; record (*Diagram D*).

- Compare your crotch measurement with the pattern crotch measurement to determine if an alteration is necessary.

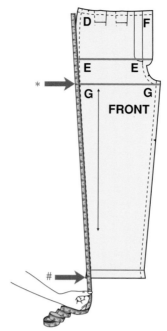

Diagram A: Keep tape measure positioned at crotch line (*); extend it to hem cutting line (#).

Diagram B: If your cutting line is above finished hemline, lay other end of tape measure so that tab end meets your measurement; read measurement from tape at cutting line.

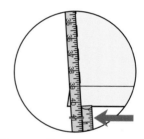

Diagram C: If your cutting line is below pattern cutting line, lay other end of tape measure so that tab meets pattern cutting line; read measurement at mark.

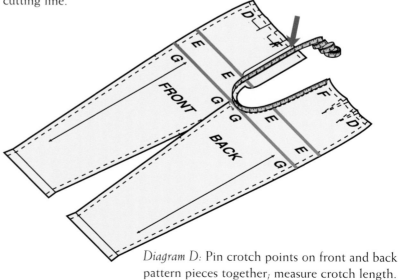

Diagram D: Pin crotch points on front and back pattern pieces together; measure crotch length.

Pattern Waist

• Fold the darts of the pattern closed at the waist seam.

• Pin the front and back pattern pieces together at the side seam, stacking stitching lines at the waist (*Diagram A*).

• Measure along the waist seam between stitching lines, standing the tape measure on the side. Double the measurement to achieve the actual width; record.

Note from Nancy: A tape measure can serve as a quick calculator. To double a measurement, fold the tape at the measured mark. The end of the tape will be at the doubled amount.

• Compare your waist measurement with the pattern waist measurement to determine if you need to make an alteration.

Pattern Hip

• Pin the pattern pieces together at the side seam, stacking stitching lines at the hip.

• Measure along the hip line between stitching lines. Double this measurement for the actual width; record (*Diagram B*).

• Compare your hip measurement with the pattern hip measurement to determine if you need to make an alteration.

Pattern Thigh

• Pin the pant pattern pieces together at the side seams, stacking stitching lines at the crotch. (The horizontal crotch line is the same as the thigh line.)

• Measure along the crotch line between stitching lines; record (*Diagram C*).

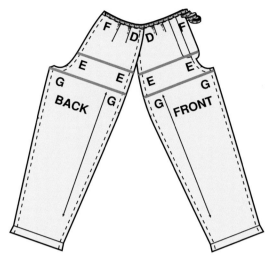

Diagram A: Fold darts closed; pin front and back pattern pieces together at side seam. Measure waist.

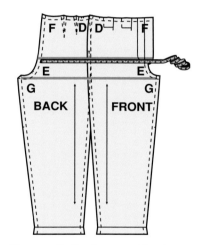

Diagram B: Pin front and back pattern pieces together at side seam; measure at hip line.

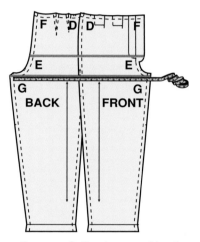

Diagram C: Pin front and back pattern pieces together; measure at crotch line.

• Compare your thigh measurement with the pattern thigh measurement to determine if you need to make an alteration.

Note from Nancy: Remember, it's only necessary to measure the pattern's thigh width if the widest area of your figure is below the hip.

First Work Sheet: Length Changes

Keep fitting simple by grouping similar activities. Start by making all length alterations on the same work sheet. Then make all width alterations on a second work sheet. Changing the length first and the width second streamlines the process. For example, if you need to change the overall length, make this the first alteration on your list. It will save both time and tracing!

Cut the work sheet longer than the pattern piece and place it under the pattern. To change the pant length, the side curve, or the crotch length, slide the pattern up or down along the grain line as you would raise or lower a window.

HEM CHANGES

Determining Changes

Refer to the fitting chart for pants (page 139) to determine the amount to alter the hem. Add or subtract the total change needed on both the front and back pattern pieces.

LENGTHENING

1. Outline the hem and 1″ of both side seams of the front pattern piece on the first work sheet.

2. Measure up from the hemline the amount the pants need to be lengthened; mark on the work sheet (*Diagram A*).

3. Slide the pattern up to the mark, following the grain line. Trace the remainder of the pattern, extending the sides down to the new hemline (*Diagram B*).

4. Match the pattern to the outline; tape. Cut out, following the new outline.

5. Repeat steps 1 through 4 on the back pattern piece (*Diagram C*).

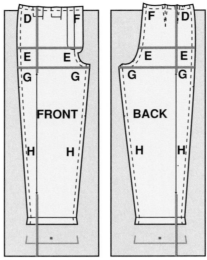

Diagram A: Outline hem and 1″ of side seam. Measure increase above hem; mark.

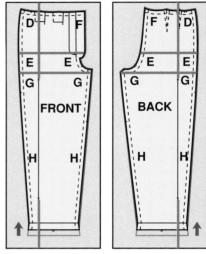

Diagram B: Slide pattern up; trace.

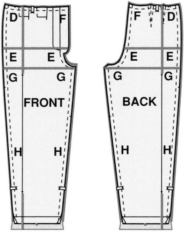

Diagram C: Completed alteration for longer hem

Sliding makes even cuffed pants easy to lengthen or to shorten.

Shortening

1. Outline the hem and 1" of both side seams of the front pattern piece on the first work sheet.

2. Measure down from the hemline the amount the pants need to be shortened; mark it on the work sheet *(Diagram A)*.

3. Slide the pattern down to the mark, following the grain line. Trace the remainder of the pattern, extending the sides to the new hemline *(Diagram B)*.

Note from Nancy: If the pants are shortened a considerable amount, the new hem could appear too wide. To keep the original width, simply draw a new cutting line from the original hem width, tapering up to meet the pattern at the knee line on both sides.

4. Match the pattern to the outline; tape. Fold in the pattern sections that overlap the new outline. Cut out, following the new outline.

5. Repeat steps 1 through 4 on the back pattern piece *(Diagram C)*.

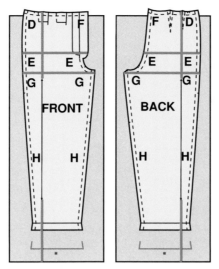

Diagram A: Outline hem and 1" of side seams. Measure decrease below hem; mark.

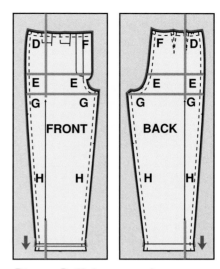

Diagram B: Slide pattern down to mark; trace.

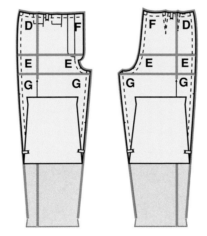

Diagram C: Completed alteration for shorter hem

SIDE CURVE FITTING TECHNIQUES

Adding length at the side adjusts for a high hip; taking away length accommodates a low, flat hip. Both fitting techniques are easily done at the side seams of the front and back pattern pieces.

LENGTHENING

Determining Changes

Refer to the fitting chart for pants on page 139 to see if any length is needed for a proper fit at the side curve. The total length needed will be added to the front and back pattern pieces.

1. Place the front pattern piece on the first work sheet. Use the same work sheet you used to alter the hem length; if no change to hem length was needed, outline the side and waist cutting lines on the work sheet. Measure up from the waist cutting line at the side seam the needed increase; mark (*Diagram A*).

2. Slide the pattern up to the mark, following the grain line. Trace the longer side cutting line (*Diagram B*).

3. Place a pin at pivot point D; pivot the pattern down to the original waist outline. Trace the new waist cutting line (*Diagram C*).

4. Match the pattern to the original outline; tape. Cut out, following the new outline.

5. Repeat steps 1 through 4 on the back pattern piece (*Diagram D*).

<u>Note from Nancy:</u> If one hip is higher than the other, alter the pattern for the higher hip. It will be easy to remove length from the shorter side during the first fitting.

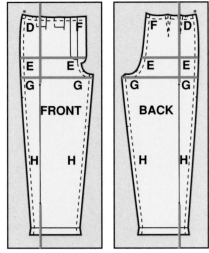

Diagram A: Outline pattern; mark increase.

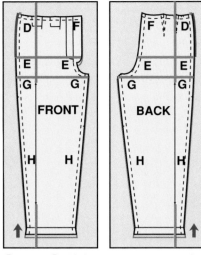

Diagram B: Slide pattern up to mark; trace longer side cutting line.

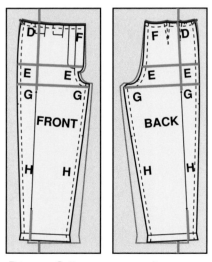

Diagram C: Pivot to original waist cutting line; trace.

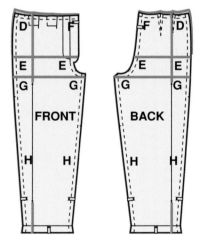

Diagram D: Completed alteration for longer side curve

Shortening

Determining Changes

Refer to the fitting chart for pants on page 139 to see if length should be subtracted at the side curve. The total amount will be subtracted from the front and back pattern pieces.

1. Place the front pattern piece on the first work sheet. Use the same work sheet you used to alter the hem length; if no change to hem length was needed, outline the side and waist cutting lines on the work sheet. Measure down from the waist cutting line at the side seam the needed decrease; mark (*Diagram A*).

2. Slide the pattern down to the mark, following the grain line (*Diagram B*).

3. Place a pin at pivot point D; pivot the pattern up to the original waist outline. Trace the new waist cutting line (*Diagram C*).

4. Match the pattern to the original outline; tape. Fold back the pattern sections that overlap the new cutting lines. Cut out, following the new outline.

5. Repeat steps 1 through 4 on the back pattern piece (*Diagram D*).

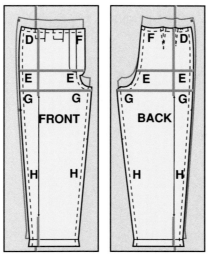

Diagram A: Outline pattern; mark decrease.

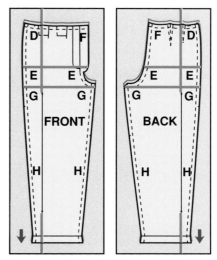

Diagram B: Slide pattern down to mark.

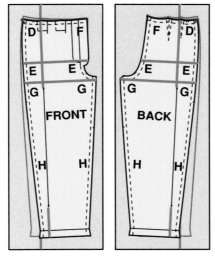

Diagram C: Pivot to original waist cutting line at center; trace.

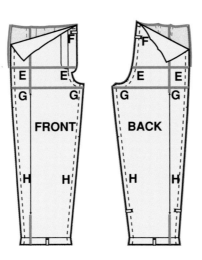

Diagram D: Completed alteration for shorter side curve

Correct side curve fit means pant creases hang straight.

CROTCH ALTERATIONS

When I think of the word *finesse*, the adjective *refinement* comes to mind. For pants Fitting Finesse, most of us need to refine the fit at the crotch. This refinement is made easy with five options. It will not be difficult to determine which option to choose—your figure type and the alteration amount will lead you in the right direction.

Note from Nancy: Pant patterns are drafted the way most of us are shaped—with a slight curve in the front and a fuller curve in the back. To give us sitting room, the back pattern is 2" to 3" longer than the front.

LENGTHENING 4" OR LESS

Determining Changes

Refer to the fitting chart for pants (page 139) for the amount to be added to the crotch area. Divide the needed alteration by two, since the amount will be added evenly to the front and the back.

1. Place the front pattern piece on the first work sheet. If this is the first alteration you are making, outline the pattern cutting lines on the work sheet. Measure down from the crotch cutting line the needed increase amount; mark (*Diagram A*).

2. Slide the pattern down to the mark, following the grain line.

3. Trace the lower part of the new crotch line and the changed portion of the inseam on the work sheet (*Diagram B*).

4. Match the pattern to the original outline; tape. Fold back the pattern sections that overlap the new cutting lines. Cut out, following the new outline.

5. Repeat steps 1 through 4 on the back pattern piece (*Diagram C*).

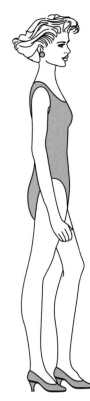

If your figure has more curve than average or you're long waisted, you'll need to add crotch length.

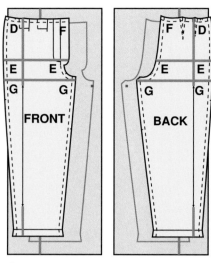

Diagram A: Outline pattern. Measure down from each crotch cutting line; mark increase.

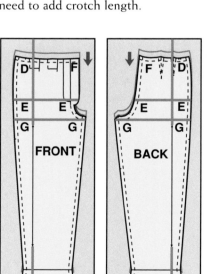

Diagram B: Slide pattern down to mark; trace new lower crotch line and changes to inseam.

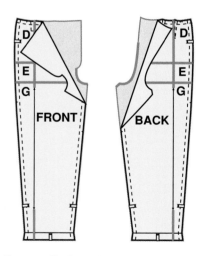

Diagram C: Completed alteration for lengthening crotch 4" or less

SHORTENING 4" OR LESS

Determining Changes

Refer to the fitting chart for pants (page 139) for the amount to be subtracted from the crotch area. Divide the needed alteration by two, since the amount will be taken evenly from the front and the back.

1. Place the front pattern piece on the first work sheet. If this is the first alteration you are making, outline the pattern cutting lines on the work sheet. Measure up from the crotch cutting line the needed decrease amount; mark (*Diagram A*).

2. Slide the pattern up to the mark, following the grain line.

3. Trace the raised part of the new crotch line and the changed portion of the inseam on the work sheet (*Diagram B*).

4. Match the pattern to the original outline; tape. Cut out, following the new outline.

5. Repeat steps 1 through 4 on the back pattern piece (*Diagram C*).

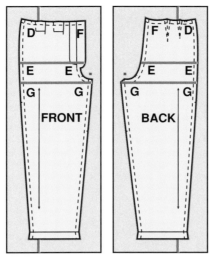

Diagram A: Outline pattern. Measure up from crotch cutting line; mark decrease.

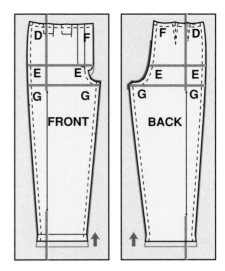

Diagram B: Slide pattern up to mark; trace new raised crotch line and changes to inseam.

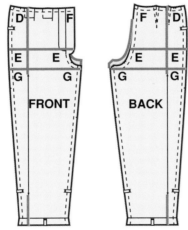

Diagram C: Completed alteration for shortening crotch 4" or less

Proper fit in crotch area is essential for good-looking pants.

LENGTHENING 4" OR MORE

If the crotch needs to be longer by 4" or more, part of the alteration is made at the crotch points and part at the center front or the center back. There are three possibilities; choose the option that best fits your shape.

Option 1: Full Figure

A full figure has a rounded tummy and a predominant seat curve. Refer to the fitting chart for pants on page 139 for the amount to add to the crotch area.

• Add 1" above the waist cutting lines at the center front and back.

• Divide the remaining increase between both the front and back crotch points. For example, if you need to add 6", add 1" above the original outline at the center front and 1" above the center back. Then lower both the front and back crotch points 2" each.

1. Place the front pattern piece on the first work sheet. If this is the first alteration for this pattern, outline the cutting lines. Measure and mark the points determined above (*Diagram A*).

2. Slide the pattern to change the crotch line.

• Lengthen the crotch by sliding the front pattern piece down to the crotch mark, following the grain line. Trace the lower part of the new crotch line and the changed portion of the inseam (*Diagram B*).

• Add waist length by sliding the pattern up to the new center front mark, following the grain line. Trace the longer crotch line. Do not move the pattern (*Diagram C*).

3. Place a pin at pivot point F; pivot the pattern out to the original side cutting line. Trace the new waist cutting line (*Diagram D*).

4. Match the pattern to the original outline; tape. Fold back the pattern sections that overlap the new outline. Cut out, following the new outline.

5. Repeat steps 1 through 4 on the back pattern piece (*Diagram E*).

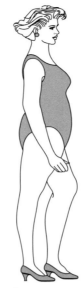

Full figures have more curve than average at both tummy and seat.

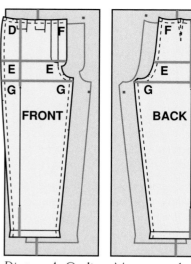

Diagram A: Outline. Measure and mark increases at waist and crotch points on center front and center back pieces.

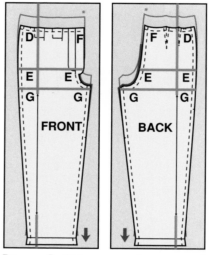

Diagram B: Slide pattern down to mark; trace.

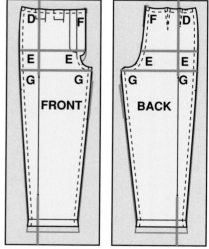

Diagram C: Slide pattern up to waist increase; trace longer crotch line.

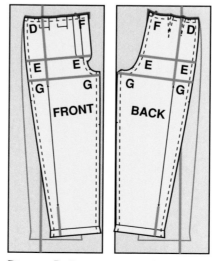

Diagram D: Pivot to original side cutting line; trace new waist cutting line.

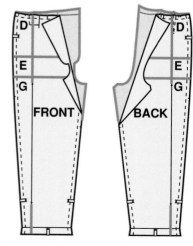

Diagram E: Completed alterations for full figure

Option 2:
Predominant Tummy

This figure type has a large curve in the tummy area and less of a curve in the seat. Refer to the fitting chart for pants on page 139 for the amount to add to the crotch area.

• Add 1″ above the waist cutting line at the center front only.

• Divide the remaining increase between both the front and back crotch points. For example, if you need to add 5″, add 1″ above the outline at the center front. Then lower both the front and back crotch points 2″ each.

1. Place the front and back pattern pieces on the first work sheets. If this is the first alteration for this pattern, outline the cutting lines. Measure and mark the points determined above (*Diagram A*).

2. Slide the front pattern piece down to the crotch mark, following the grain line. Trace the lower part of the crotch line and the changed portion of the inseam. Repeat on the back pattern piece (*Diagram B*).

3. Slide the front pattern piece up along the grain line to the center front mark. Trace the longer crotch line. Do not move the pattern (*Diagram C*).

4. Place a pin at pivot point F; pivot the front pattern piece in to the original side cutting line. Trace the new waist cutting line (*Diagram D*).

5. Match the pattern pieces to the original outline and tape. Fold back the pattern sections that overlap the new outline. Cut out, following the new outline (*Diagram E*).

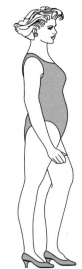

If you have more curve in tummy than in seat, add length to front.

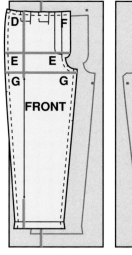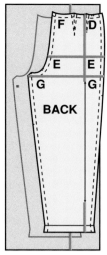

Diagram A: Outline. Mark increases at front waist and both crotch points.

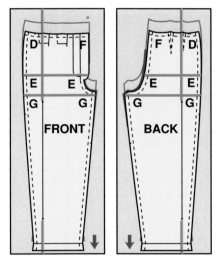

Diagram B: Slide pattern down to mark; trace.

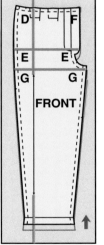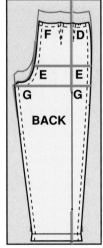

Diagram C: Slide front pattern piece up to center front mark; trace longer crotch line.

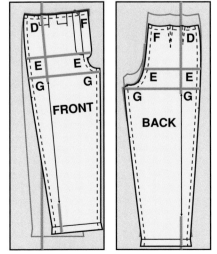

Diagram D: Pivot to original side cutting line; trace new waist cutting line.

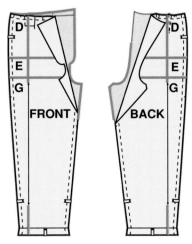

Diagram E: Completed alterations for predominant tummy

Option 3: Predominant Seat

This figure type has a greater curve in the seat area. Refer to the fitting chart for pants on page 139 for the amount to add to the crotch area.

• Add 1″ above the waist cutting line at the center back only.

• Divide the remaining increase between both the front and back crotch points. For example, if you need to add 7″, add 1″ above the outline at the center back. Then lower both the front and back crotch points 3″ each.

1. Place the front and back pattern pieces on the first work sheets. If this is the first alteration for this pattern, outline the cutting lines. Measure and mark the points determined above (*Diagram A*).

2. Slide the front and back pattern pieces down to the new crotch marks, following the grain line. Trace the lower part of the crotch line and the changed portion of the inseam (*Diagram B*).

3. Add waist length to the back pattern piece by sliding the pattern up along the grain line to the center back mark. Trace the longer crotch line. Do not move the pattern (*Diagram C*).

4. Place a pin at pivot point F; pivot the back pattern piece in to the original side cutting line. Trace the new waist cutting line (*Diagram D*).

5. Match both pattern pieces to the original outlines; tape. Fold back the pattern sections that overlap the new outline. Cut out, following the new outline (*Diagram E*).

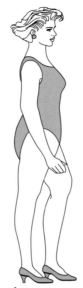

If your figure has more seat curve than average, add extra back length.

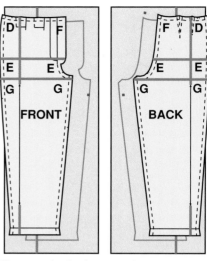

Diagram A: Outline. Mark increases at back waist and both crotch points.

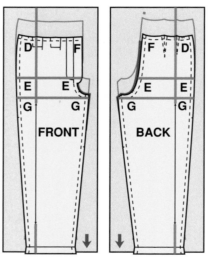

Diagram B: Slide down to crotch mark; trace.

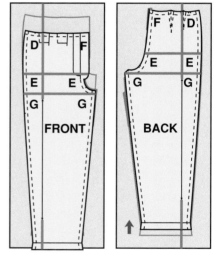

Diagram C: Slide back pattern piece to waist mark; trace longer back crotch line.

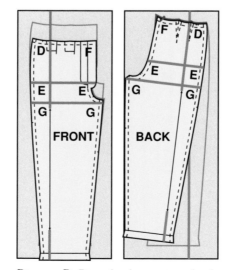

Diagram D: Pivot back to original side cutting line; trace new waist cutting line.

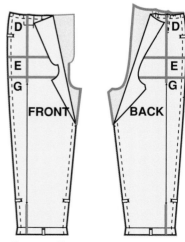

Diagram E: Completed alterations for predominant seat

Second Work Sheet: Width Changes

Three width alterations are made by simply pivoting the pattern. The pattern is anchored with a pin and can be moved like the pendulum of a clock to add or to subtract inches.

All length changes were made on one work sheet and all width changes can be made on a second work sheet. Cut out the first work sheet with the length changes, following the new cutting lines. Match the pattern to the original outline and tape the pattern to the work sheet. Fold in any pattern sections that overlap the new outline.

The combination of the original pattern and the first work sheet becomes your new pattern. Use this new pattern as your guideline for outlining width changes (*Diagram A*).

For ease in pivoting for width changes, the directions are given separately for waist, hip, and thigh alterations. At the end of the chapter, several common alteration combinations are given. If you need two or more width changes, read through the individual alterations and then refer to the end of the chapter for the appropriate combination.

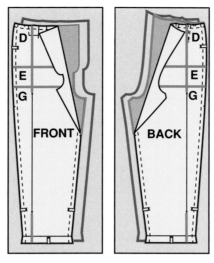

Diagram A: First work sheet becomes pattern for making width changes.

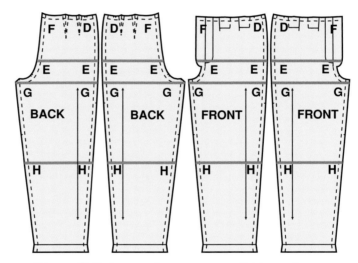

Diagram B: Eight cut edges mean you divide total amount to add or to subtract by eight.

FITTING THE WAIST

Determining Changes

Refer to the fitting chart for pants (page 139) for the amount to alter the waist. Divide the waist alteration amount by eight (the number of cut edges on the four seams).

Note from Nancy: Use this fraction trick to figure the amount: Place the needed number of inches over eight. For example, to add 5" to the waist, add ⅝" at each cut edge. If you need 3", the amount to add is ⅜" at each cut edge (*Diagram B*).

Add the divided increase to the waist on both the front and back pattern pieces. Subtract the divided decrease from the waist on both the front and back pattern pieces.

INCREASING

1. Place the front pattern piece on the second work sheet. Outline the cutting lines. Measure the needed increase out on both sides of the waist cutting line; mark (*Diagram A*).

Note from Nancy: As a reminder, if you made length changes, the first work sheet is used as the pattern. If you didn't make any length changes, use the original pattern.

2. Alter the side seam.
• Place a pin at side seam pivot point E; pivot the pattern out to the increase mark. Trace the new cutting line between the waist and the hip.
• Extend the waist cutting line to the new width (*Diagram B*).
• Match the pattern to the original outline.

3. Alter the center seam.
• Place a pin at center seam pivot point E; pivot the pattern out to the increase mark. Trace the new cutting line between the waist and the hip (*Diagram C*).
• Extend the waist cutting line to the new width.

4. Match the pattern to the original outline; tape. Cut out, following the new outline.

5. Repeat steps 1 through 4 on the back pattern piece (*Diagram D*).

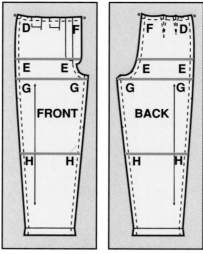

Diagram A: Outline pattern. Measure increase; mark on both sides.

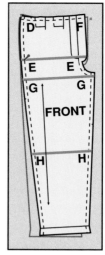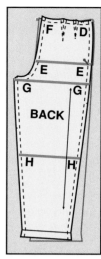

Diagram B: Pivot to increase on side seam; trace new cutting line between waist and hip.

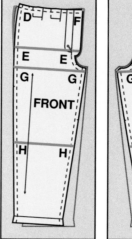

Diagram C: Pivot to increase at center seam; trace new center cutting line.

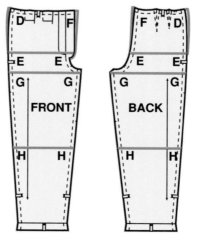

Diagram D: Completed alteration for larger waist

Pants with fitted waist

DECREASING

1. Place the front pattern piece on the second work sheet. Outline the cutting lines. Measure in from both sides of the waist cutting line; mark (*Diagram A*).

2. Alter the side seam.

• Place a pin at side seam pivot point E; pivot the pattern in to the decrease mark. Trace the new cutting line between the waist and the hip (*Diagram B*).

• Match the pattern piece to the original outline.

3. Alter the center seam.

• Place a pin at center seam pivot point E; pivot the pattern in to the decrease mark.

• Trace the new cutting line between the waist and the hip (*Diagram C*).

4. Match the pattern to the original outline; tape. Fold back the pattern sections that overlap the new outline. Cut out, following the new outline.

5. Repeat steps 1 through 4 on the back pattern piece (*Diagram D*).

Note from Nancy: See "Altering the Waistband" on page 76.

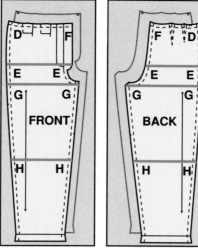

Diagram A: Outline pattern. Measure in needed decrease from both sides of waist cutting line; mark.

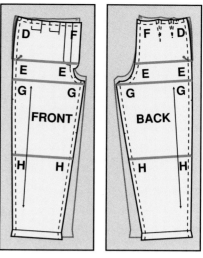

Diagram B: Pivot to decrease mark at side seam; trace new cutting line between waist and hip.

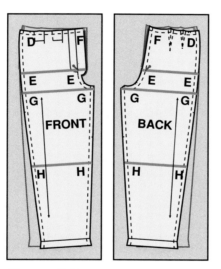

Diagram C: Pivot to increase mark at center seam; trace new center cutting line.

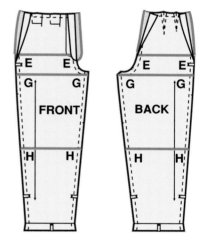

Diagram D: Completed alteration for smaller waist

FITTING THE HIP

If you purchased a pattern smaller than your hip measurement (using the chart on page 90), you will need to increase the hip of your pattern. The change is easy, and the fit you'll achieve will be worth the time spent making this simple alteration.

Determining Changes

Refer to the fitting chart for pants (page 139) to determine the amount to alter the hip. Divide the alteration amount by eight (the number of cut edges on the four seams).

1. Place the front pattern piece on the second work sheet. If this is the first width alteration for this pattern, outline the pattern. Measure the needed increase out on both sides of the hip cutting lines; mark (*Diagram A*).

2. Alter the side seam.

• Place a pin at side seam pivot point H; pivot the pattern out to the increase mark. Trace the new cutting line between the knee and the hip. Do not move the pattern (*Diagram B*).

• Move the pin to side seam pivot point E; pivot the pattern to the original waist outline. Trace the new cutting line between the hip and the waist (*Diagram C*). Match the pattern piece to the original outline.

3. Alter the inseam and the center seam.

• Place a pin at inseam pivot point H; pivot the pattern out to the increase mark. Trace the new cutting line between the knee and the hip. Keep the pattern pivoted (*Diagram D*).

• Move the pin to center seam pivot point E; pivot the pattern to the original outline at the waist. Trace the new cutting line between the hip and the waist (*Diagram E*).

4. Match the pattern to the original outline; tape. Cut out, following the new outline.

5. Repeat steps 1 through 4 on the back pattern piece (*Diagram F*).

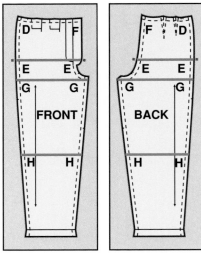

Diagram A: Outline front pattern piece, measure increase on both sides of hip cutting lines; mark.

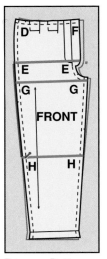

Diagram B: Pivot to increase on side cutting line; trace.

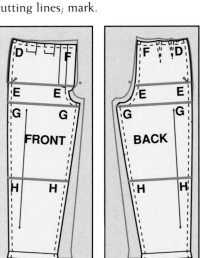

Diagram C: Pivot to waist; trace new cutting line between hip and waist.

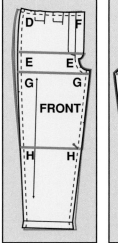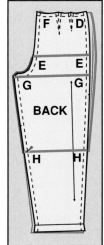

Diagram D: Pivot to increase at inseam; trace new cutting line between knee and hip.

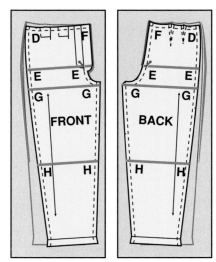

Diagram E: Pivot to waist; trace between hip and waist.

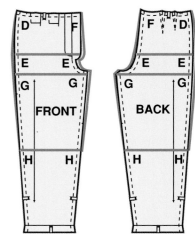

Diagram F: Completed alteration for larger hip

FITTING THE THIGH

Using the chart on page 90, you bought a pattern smaller than your hip to give a better fit in the thigh and the crotch. For that reason, you should not need to decrease the thigh. (Remember, it's easier to make a pattern larger than smaller.)

Determining Changes

Refer to the fitting chart for pants on page 139 to determine the amount to add to the thigh. Divide the increase by four (the number of seam edges in each pant leg).

1. Place the front pattern piece on the second work sheet. If this is the first width alteration, outline the pattern. Measure the needed increase at the cutting line on each end of the crotch line; mark (*Diagram A*).

2. Alter the side seam.

• Place a pin at side seam pivot point H; pivot the pattern out to the increase mark. Trace the new cutting line between the knee and the crotch mark. Keep the pattern pivoted (*Diagram B*).

• Move the pin to side seam pivot point G; pivot the pattern to the waist outline. Trace the new cutting line between the crotch and the waist (*Diagram C*). Match the pattern piece to the original outline.

3. Alter the inseam and the center seam.

• Place the pin at inseam pivot point H; pivot the pattern piece to the increase mark. Trace the new cutting line between the knee and the crotch. Keep the pattern pivoted (*Diagram D*).

• Move the pin to inseam pivot point G; pivot the pattern to the waist outline. Trace the new cutting line between the crotch and the waist (*Diagram E*).

4. Match the pattern to the original outline; tape. Cut out, following the new outline.

5. Repeat steps 1 through 4 on the back pattern piece (*Diagram F*).

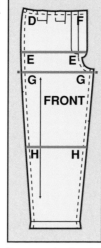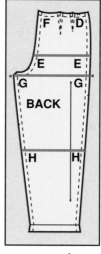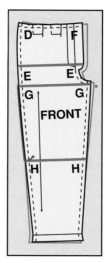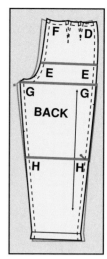

Diagram A: Outline pattern; mark increase on both ends of crotch line.

Diagram B: Pivot to increase mark at crotch line; trace new cutting line between knee and crotch.

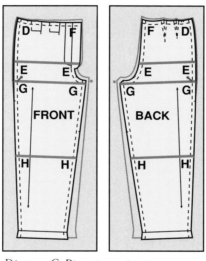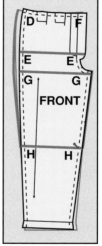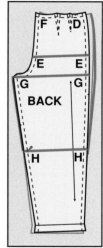

Diagram C: Pivot to waist; trace new cutting line between crotch and waist.

Diagram D: Pivot to increase mark on the inseam; trace new cutting line between knee and crotch.

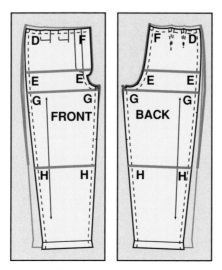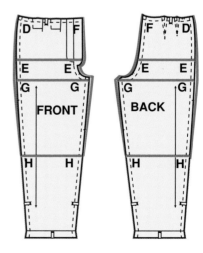

Diagram E: Pivot to waist; trace new cutting line between crotch and waist.

Diagram F: Completed alteration for larger thigh

Width Combinations

INCREASED WAIST AND HIP

Fitting Finesse makes combining alterations quick. One of the most common combinations involves increasing both the waist and the hip.

Determining Changes

Refer to the fitting chart for pants on page 139 for the amounts to increase the waist and the hip. Divide the amounts by eight.

1. Place the front pattern piece on the second work sheet; outline the pattern. Measure the needed increases out on both sides of the hip and both sides of the waist cutting lines; mark (*Diagram A*).

2. Alter the side seam.

• Place a pin at side seam pivot point H; pivot the pattern out to the hip increase mark. Trace the new cutting line between the knee and the hip. Keep the pattern pivoted (*Diagram B*).

• Move the pin to side seam pivot point E; pivot the pattern to the waist increase mark. Trace the new cutting line between the hip and the waist.

• Extend the waist cutting line to the new width (*Diagram C*).

• Match the pattern to the original outline.

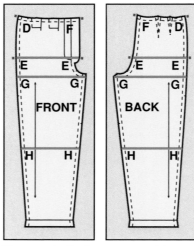

Diagram A: Outline pattern. Measure needed increase on both sides of hip and both sides of waist; mark.

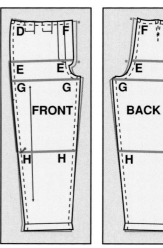

Diagram B: Pivot to hip increase at side seam; trace new cutting line between knee and hip.

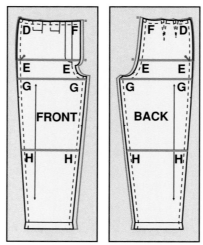

Diagram C: Pivot to waist increase at side seam; trace new cutting line between hip and waist. Extend waist cutting line.

Streamline fitting by combining alterations on one work sheet.

3. Alter the inseam and the center seam.

• Place a pin at inseam pivot point H; pivot the pattern out to the hip increase mark. Trace the new cutting line between the knee and the hip. Keep the pattern pivoted (*Diagram D*).

• Move the pin to center seam line pivot point E; pivot the pattern to the waist increase mark. Trace the new cutting line between the hip and the waist.

• Extend the waist cutting line to meet the new width (*Diagram E*).

4. Match the pattern to the original outline; tape. Cut out, following the new outline.

5. Repeat steps 1 through 4 on the back pattern piece (*Diagram F*).

Note from Nancy: If you need to increase the hip and decrease the waist, simply pivot in to the waist decrease mark. It's that simple!

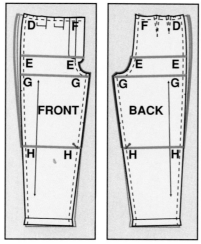

Diagram D: Pivot to hip increase at inseam; trace new cutting line from knee to hip.

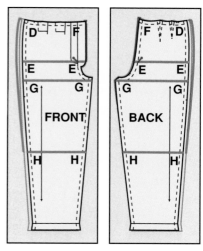

Diagram E: Pivot to waist increase at center seam; trace new cutting line from hip to waist. Extend waist cutting line.

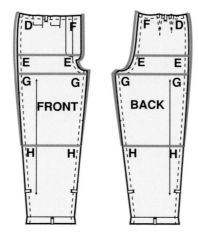

Diagram F: Completed alterations for larger waist and hip

INCREASED WAIST, HIP, AND THIGH

When you use the Fitting Finesse Pant Pattern Size Chart on page 90 to choose your pattern size, you may need to increase at the waist, the hip, and the thigh. This is certain to be the case if your hip measurement is greater than 50″, since I recommend against buying patterns larger than Misses' size 22. Don't worry, though, because pivot-and-slide techniques make this triple combination easy.

Determining Changes

Refer to the fitting chart for pants on page 139 for the amounts to increase. Divide the needed increase for the thigh by four (four cut edges per two seams in each pant leg) and divide the needed increases for the waist and the hip by eight.

1. Place the front pattern piece on the second work sheet; outline the pattern. Measure and mark the needed increases on both sides of the crotch (for the thigh), hip, and waist cutting lines (*Diagram A*).

2. Alter the side seam.

• Place a pin at side seam pivot point H; pivot the pattern out to the increase mark at the crotch line. Trace the new cutting line between the knee and the crotch. Keep the pattern pivoted (*Diagram B*).

• Move the pin to side seam pivot point G; pivot the pattern to the increase mark at the hip. Trace the new cutting line between the crotch and the hip; keep the pattern pivoted (*Diagram C*).

• Move the pin to side seam pivot point E; pivot the pattern to the increase mark at the waist. Trace the new cutting line between the hip and the waist (*Diagram D*).

• Move the pattern back to the original outline.

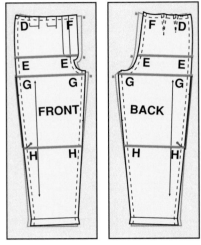

Diagram A: Outline pattern. Measure needed increases on both sides of crotch (thigh), hip, and waist cutting lines; mark.

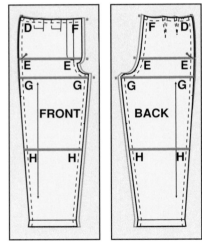

Diagram B: Pivot to increase at crotch line; trace new cutting line between knee and crotch.

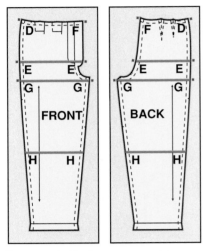

Diagram C: Pivot to hip increase at side seam; trace new cutting line between crotch and hip.

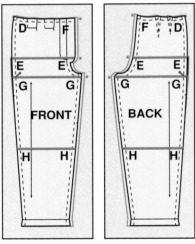

Diagram D: Pivot to waist increase at side seam; trace new cutting line between hip and waist.

3. Alter the inseam and the center seam.

• Place a pin at inseam pivot point H; pivot the pattern out to the increase mark at the crotch line. Trace the new cutting line between the knee and the crotch mark. Keep the pattern piece pivoted (*Diagram E*).

• Move the pin to inseam pivot point G; pivot the pattern to the increase mark at the hip. Trace the new cutting line between the crotch and the hip. Keep the pattern pivoted (*Diagram F*).

• Move the pin to center seam pivot point E; pivot the pattern to the increase mark at the waist. Trace the new cutting line between the hip and the waist (*Diagram G*).

4. Match the pattern to the original outline; tape. Cut out, following the new outline.

5. Repeat steps 1 through 4 on the back pattern piece (*Diagram H*).

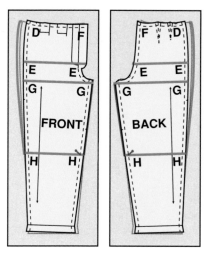

Diagram E: Pivot to crotch increase at inseam; trace new cutting line between knee and crotch.

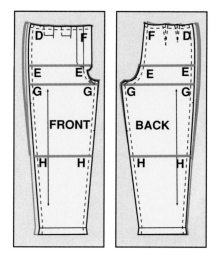

Diagram F: Pivot to increase mark at center seam; trace new cutting line between crotch and hip.

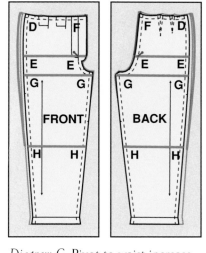

Diagram G: Pivot to waist increase mark at center seam; trace new cutting line between hip and waist.

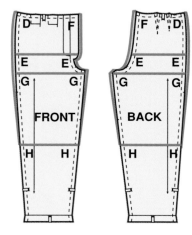

Diagram H: Completed alterations for larger waist, hip, and thigh

Fitting Finesse works especially well for fitting pants for large or small figures.

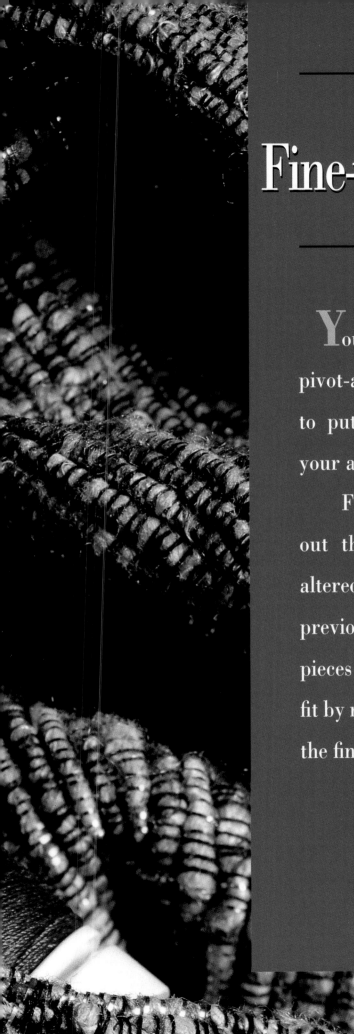

Fine-tuning the $\mathcal{F}$it

You've custom-fit your pattern with pivot-and-slide techniques. Now it's time to put the garment together and check your alterations.

Fine-tuning the fit is simple. First, cut out the classic-style garment that you altered using the instructions given in a previous chapter. Then baste the fabric pieces together in key areas and adjust the fit by removing unwanted wrinkles. This is the final stage of Fitting Finesse!

PATTERN PIVOT POINTS

The fine-tuning steps in this chapter sometimes refer to pivot points. Here's a quick reminder of what those points are for each type of garment. If you're fine-tuning the fit on a specialty pattern (one with dolman sleeves, dropped shoulders, raglan sleeves, or princess seams) refer to page 55 or page 63 for details of marking pivot points.

Blouses, Dresses, and Jackets

A—Point where neck and shoulder stitching lines cross

B—Point where shoulder and armhole stitching lines cross

C—Point where armhole and side seam stitching lines cross

D—Point where waistline crosses side seam stitching line

E—Point where hip and side seam stitching lines cross

Sleeves

B—Point on stitching line at large dot at cap of sleeve

C—Points where armhole and underarm stitching lines cross at both sides of sleeve

Skirts

D—Point where waist and side seam stitching lines cross

E—Point where hip line crosses side seam stitching line

F—Point where center front/back intersects waist stitching line

Pants

D—Point where waist and side seam stitching lines cross

E—Points where hip line crosses stitching lines at center seam and at side seam

F—Point where center front and waist stitching lines cross

G—Points where crotch line crosses stitching line at inseam and at side seam

H—Points where knee line crosses stitching line at inseam and at side seam

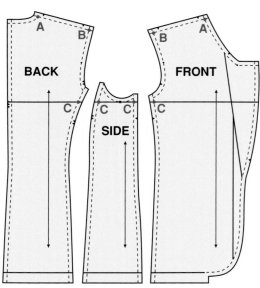

Three-piece jacket pivot points

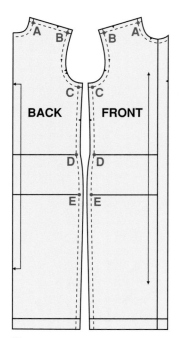

Dress pivot points

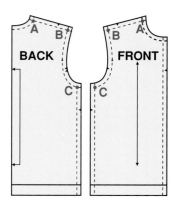

Blouse pivot points

DRAWING REFERENCE LINES

When instructions call for extending the grain line or adding a reference line such as at the hip line, use a yardstick and a marking pen to draw on the pattern piece. Transfer the line to the work sheet by using a tracing wheel. Place the pattern on top of the work sheet; trace along the line. The tracing wheel points will perforate the work sheet, producing a guideline.

Grain Lines

Extend the grain line the full length of the pattern and the work sheet to make it easier to slide the pattern up and down when changing length.

Hip Line

For a hip line, measure down from the waistline on the pattern piece the amount of your hipline length. (See page 11 for how to take this measurement.) Draw this reference line directly on the pattern front and back.

Pant Reference Lines

Three lines perpendicular to the grain line help you locate pant pivot points.

Crotch line begins at the point where the crotch and inseam stitching lines cross.

Hip line is 2″ above the crotch line.

Knee line is located midway between the crotch line and the hemline.

FINE-TUNING ADVANTAGES

Once the garment is basted together, check the fit by "reading" and removing any wrinkles that appear in your problem areas.

While this process of checking for wrinkles may seem time-consuming, it's actually going to save you time in the future in three ways.

1. This is the only fit-check you need for this garment. The wrinkles are easy to eliminate, and once you transfer what you learn from the garment to the pattern, you can complete the garment.

2. After you make the corrections on your classic-style pattern, you can reuse it without checking the fit.

3. Best of all, you can make the same changes automatically on any pattern in the same size from the same company, without further measuring. For example, if you increased the bust and narrowed the shoulders on a Misses' size 12 McCall's dress, on the next size 12 top or jacket pattern from McCall's, you would make the same changes.

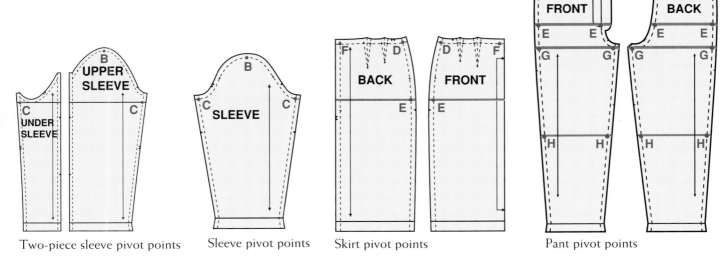

Two-piece sleeve pivot points   Sleeve pivot points   Skirt pivot points   Pant pivot points

Checking the Fit

Throughout this book, I've asked you to use a classic-style pattern for your first pivot-and-slide alteration project. That's because this simple styling makes it easy to check the fit.

MACHINE-BASTING FABRIC PIECES

After cutting the pattern, machine-baste the basic pieces together. Use a machine-basting stitch and slightly loosen the top tension to make removing the stitches an easy process. Use the order given below.

For blouses, dresses, and jackets *(Diagrams A, B, and C)*:
- Darts
- Shoulder seams
- Center front or center back and side seams
- Sleeve underarm seam
- Armhole seam for set-in sleeves

For skirts *(Diagram D)*:
- Pleats, darts, or gathers
- Center front, center back, and side seams (Do not close zipper opening.)

For pants *(Diagram E)*:
- Pleats, darts, or gathers
- Inseams
- Center front and center back crotch (Do not close zipper opening.)
- Side seams

Diagram A: Machine-basted blouse

Diagram B: Machine-basted dress

Diagram C: Machine-basted jacket

Diagram D: Machine-basted skirt

Diagram E: Machine-basted pants

TRYING ON THE GARMENT

Note from Nancy: Have your sewing buddy help you fine-tune the fit. If you have to work alone, do the best you can. Remember, any improvement will make your garment fit better than most ready-to-wear clothes.

For blouses, tops, jackets, and dresses:
• Pin the shoulder pads in place if required.
• Try on the garment, pinning closed the center front or center back opening (*Diagram A*).

For skirts and pants:
• Using a safety pin, pin a length of 1"-wide elastic together to fit your waist.
• Pin the skirt or the pants to the elastic, matching the ⅝" waist stitching line to the center of the elastic (*Diagrams B and C*).

Diagram A: Pin in shoulder pads; pin garment closed at center front

Diagram B: Pin elastic to fit waist and pin garment to elastic.

Diagram C: Pin garment to elastic.

Checking for Wrinkles

If your garment has fitting problems, they will show up as wrinkles when you try it on. Before analyzing the fit of your garment, it is important to understand the different types of wrinkles.

Most sewing books group wrinkles into just three categories: horizontal, vertical, and bias. However, before you look at their direction, it is more useful to determine whether the wrinkles are actually folds of excess fabric or pulls caused by too little fabric. This means that there are actually six types of wrinkles, not three.

After identifying the wrinkles, alter the garment and the pattern pieces, using the instructions detailed in this chapter. To help you understand how these fine-tuning changes are made, I have used one example from each of the six wrinkle categories.

HORIZONTAL FOLD WRINKLES

A horizontal fold wrinkle occurs when there is too much length in a pattern. A common horizontal fold wrinkle occurs on skirts or pants directly below the back waist, indicating a swayback.

1. Measure the extra fold of the fabric and record.

• Pinch and pin the extra fold of fabric below the waist (*Diagram A*).

• Measure the depth of the wrinkle at the deepest part; double this measurement to determine the total wrinkle amount (*Diagram B*).

• Record the wrinkle amount on your Personal Fitting Chart for Pants (page 139) in the special measurements column.

WRINKLE CHART		
Horizontal	Horizontal fold wrinkles = too much length	Horizontal pull wrinkles = not enough width
Vertical	Vertical fold wrinkles = too much width	Vertical pull wrinkles = not enough length
Bias	Bias fold wrinkles (combine vertical and horizontal) = too much length and width	Bias pull wrinkles (combine vertical and horizontal) = not enough length and width

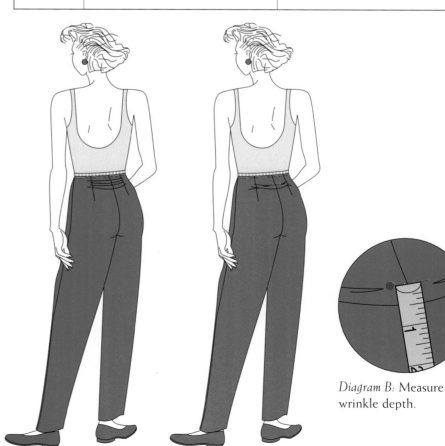

Horizontal fold wrinkles   *Diagram A:* Pin extra fabric below waist.

Diagram B: Measure wrinkle depth.

2. Take off the garment; remove the basting stitches and the pins.

3. Alter the fabric pieces.

• Fold the pant back in half with right sides together. Measure the wrinkle amount (see Step 1) down from the cutting edge at the center back; place a pin in the fabric at this point.

• Place the pant back pattern piece on top of the actual pant back; slide the pattern down until the cutting line meets the pin (*Diagram C*).

• At the center back of the pattern, insert a pin at pivot point F; pivot the pattern to the waist cutting line at the side seam (*Diagram D*).

• Trim the excess fabric, following the pattern cutting line. Save this fabric (*Diagram E*).

4. Use the fabric as a template to make the same adjustment on the pattern piece (*Diagram F*).

5. Alter all patterns of future sewing projects for a swayback.

Note from Nancy: If you notice this horizontal fold wrinkle after the waistband has been attached (or in a ready-to-wear garment), you can still correct it. Clip the back waist stitches between the side seams and make the alterations. If the garment has a zipper, bar-tack on each side just below the new cut edge and trim the excess zipper.

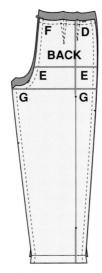

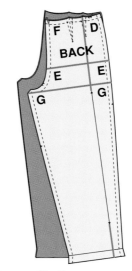

Diagram C: Slide pattern down to pin.

Diagram D: Pivot pattern to waist cutting line.

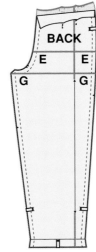

Diagram E: Trim excess fabric.

Diagram F: Use excess fabric as template to make same adjustment on pattern.

Horizontal Pull Wrinkles

Horizontal wrinkles that pull show that a garment is too tight. It is common to find these wrinkles at the bust, the waist, or the hip.

1. Clip the side seam basting stitches between the waist and the hem.

2. Restitch the seam by machine-basting a ¼" to ⅜" seam allowance. This will add 1" to 1½".

3. Try on the pants. If you still have wrinkles, sew a shallower seam using 15 stitches per inch. Zigzag or serge the edges together; press the seam allowance to one side.

4. Measure; record the hip changes on the fitting chart for pants, page 139.

5. Mark the new stitching line on the pattern pieces (*Diagram A*). For future sewing projects, increase the hip as detailed on page 80 for skirts or page 110 for pants.

Note from Nancy: When adding room to the hip of a skirt, be sure to add the same increase all the way to the hem. If you take a narrower seam allowance just at the hip, the grain line will be distorted, causing the skirt to curve in at the bottom, which emphasizes the hip.

Vertical Fold Wrinkles

Vertical fold wrinkles indicate that the pattern is too wide. A common example of a vertical fold wrinkle occurs across the back shoulder.

Note from Nancy: It's difficult to fit the back by yourself. Call on your sewing buddy to help.

1. Measure the fold and record.

• Pinch and pin the extra fold of fabric on each side of the back (*Diagram AA*).

Horizontal pull wrinkles

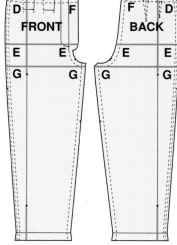

Diagram A: Mark new stitching line.

Vertical fold wrinkles

Diagram AA: Pin excess fabric from wrinkles.

- Measure the deepest part of the wrinkle; double this measurement to determine the total wrinkle amount, which you will remove from each side of the armhole area.

- Record the measurement on the fitting chart (page 141).

2. Take off the garment; remove the basting stitches and the pins.

3. Alter the fabric pieces.

- Fold the back fabric pieces with right sides together. At the center of the armhole on the garment, measure the wrinkle amount in from the cut edge (see Step 1); mark with a pin.

- Measure the same distance in from the cut edge at the underarm; mark with a pin (*Diagram BB*).

- Place the back pattern piece on top of the fabric; mark pivot point BB at the center of the armhole.

- Place a pin at pivot point B; pivot the pattern in to the marking pin at the center of the armhole.

- Remove the pin. With a fabric marking pen, trace the new cutting line on the fabric between the shoulder and the center of the armhole (*Diagram CC*).

- Keeping the pattern pivoted, move the pin to pivot point BB; pivot the pattern out to the marking pin at the underarm. Trace the remainder of the armhole cutting line on the fabric between the center of the armhole and the underarm. Remove the pin (*Diagram DD*).

- Insert a pin at pivot point C; pivot the pattern out to the cut edge of the fabric at the waist. Trace the new cutting line on the fabric from the underarm to the waist (*Diagram EE*).

4. Use the fabric piece as a template to make the same adjustment on the pattern piece (*Diagram FF*).

5. Alter all patterns of future projects for a narrow back.

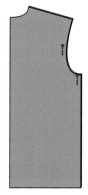

Diagram BB: Measure wrinkle depth in from armhole; mark with pins.

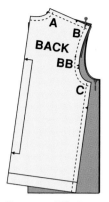

Diagram CC: Pivot to marking pin at armhole center; trace new cutting line from shoulder to armhole center.

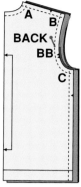

Diagram DD: Pivot to pin at underarm; trace remainder of armhole.

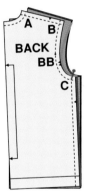

Diagram EE: Pivot at underarm; trace new cutting line from underarm to waist.

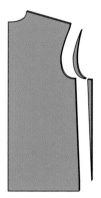

Diagram FF: Trim excess fabric; use as template to adjust pattern.

VERTICAL PULL WRINKLES

Common vertical pull wrinkles occur along the center back, indicating that the back length is too short.

1. Clip the waist stitches.

2. Sew a narrower seam allowance at the waist, tapering to a normal seam allowance at the side seams.

3. Measure and record changes on the fitting chart on page 141.

4. Mark the needed change on the pattern piece (*Diagram A*).

5. For future sewing projects, alter the pattern piece for a longer back length as detailed in "Curved Back," page 44.

BIAS FOLD WRINKLES

Bias fold wrinkles indicate too much length and width. One example is when the shoulder seam is too wide and the underarm seam is too long. Have your sewing buddy help you pinch and pin the wrinkles in this area.

1. Measure the extra folds of fabric and record.

• Pinch and pin the extra folds of fabric at the shoulder seam (vertical) and the underarm (horizontal) on the garment front (*Diagram AA*).

• Measure the depth of one vertical fold wrinkle; double the measurement for the total vertical wrinkle amount per side.

• Measure the depth of one horizontal fold wrinkle; double the measurement to determine the total horizontal wrinkle amount per side.

• Record both amounts (vertical and horizontal) on the fitting chart, page 141.

• Repeat Step 1 to measure wrinkle folds for the garment back.

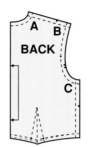

Vertical pull wrinkles

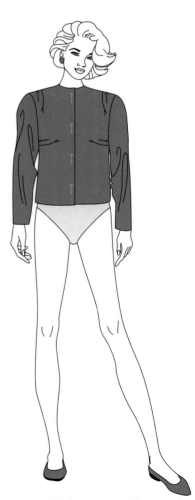

Diagram A: Mark narrower waist seam allowance on pattern.

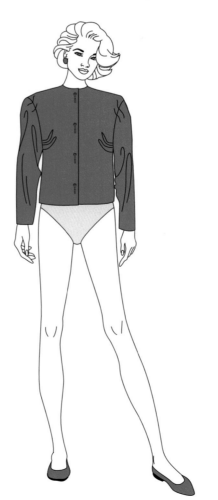

Bias fold wrinkles

Diagram AA: Pin excess fabric at shoulders and underarms.

2. Take off the garment; remove the basting stitches and the pins.

3. Alter the fabric.

• Fold the fabric front in half with right sides together.

• Measure the vertical wrinkle amount in from the end of the shoulder cutting line; place a pin vertically in the fabric at this point.

• Measure the horizontal wrinkle amount down from the cutting line at the end of the shoulder; place a pin horizontally in the fabric at this point (*Diagram BB*).

• Place the front pattern piece on top of the fabric. Slide the pattern along the shoulder cutting line until the cutting line at the end of the shoulder meets the vertical marking pin (*Diagram CC*).

• Place a pin at pivot point A; pivot the pattern to the horizontal marking pin at the end of the shoulder. Using a fabric marking pen, trace the new shoulder cutting line (*Diagram DD*).

Note from Nancy: If you're shortening more than 5/8", your pivot pin will be off the fabric. Simply move the pivot pin in (perpendicular to the grain line) until you reach the fabric stitching line and pivot from this point.

• Keeping the pattern pivoted, place a pin at pivot point B; pivot the pattern to the actual cut fabric at the underarm. Trace the new armhole cutting line with a fabric marking pen (*Diagram EE*).

4. Use the fabric piece as a template to make the same adjustment on the pattern piece (*Diagram FF*).

5. For future sewing projects, alter the pattern for narrow shoulders (page 37) and for sloping shoulders (page 40).

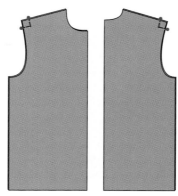

Diagram BB: Mark changes with pins at shoulder and armhole.

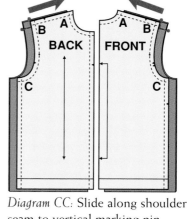

Diagram CC: Slide along shoulder seam to vertical marking pin.

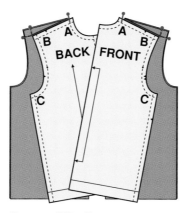

Diagram DD: Pivot; trace new shoulder cutting line.

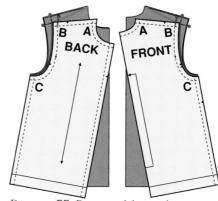

Diagram EE: Pivot to fabric edge at underarm seam; trace new armhole cutting line.

Diagram FF: Trim excess fabric; use as template to adjust pattern.

Bias Pull Wrinkles

A common bias pull wrinkle occurs below the waist, indicating that one hip is higher than the other.

1. Ask your sewing buddy to help you unpin the skirt from the elastic around your waist and clip the side seam stitches until you have eliminated the wrinkles.

2. Sew a narrower side seam (*Diagram A*). Mark a narrower waist seam on the front and the back of the higher hip side (the side with the wrinkles).

3. Measure and record the changes on the fitting chart on page 141.

4. Mark the new stitching lines on the front and back pattern pieces, noting the side with the higher hip (*Diagram B*).

5. For future sewing projects, alter the pattern for a high hip as described on page 82.

Bias pull wrinkles

Diagram A: Sew narrower side seam on higher hip side.

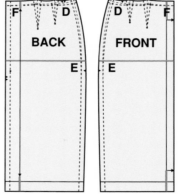

Diagram B: Mark narrower waist and side seams on pattern.

Fine-tuning the Fit in Pants

The examples used to detail the six common wrinkles apply to fitting pants, yet fine-tuning the fit in pants is generally more of a challenge than fitting other garments.

Pant wrinkles, especially in the crotch area, aren't always evident until the pants are sewn. Here are a few more wrinkle-solving alternatives to use during the fine-tuning stage or even after the pants are completed.

CROTCH WRINKLES

Horizontal folds under the seat are probably the most common wrinkle in pants. This wrinkle indicates that the inseam length is too long and the crotch length is too short. The following steps will help you easily remove these wrinkles.

1. Turn the pants wrong side out; stitch a deeper crotch seam. Sew a ½" deeper seam where the crotch curves, both on the front and the back; trim the excess seam allowance.

2. Try on your pants. If you still see a wrinkle, repeat Step 1 with a ¼" deeper seam allowance.

3. Record the change on the fitting chart for pants, page 139.

4. Mark the changes on the pattern pieces (*Diagram*).

5. On future projects, lengthen the crotch as detailed beginning on page 102.

Horizontal fold wrinkles under seat

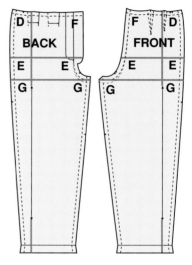

Diagram: Mark ½" deeper seam in crotch curve.

CORRECTING UNEVEN FRONT CREASES

Hanging Inward

If the side length is too long, the center front creases will bow in.

1. Unpin the pants from the elastic at the side seam, smooth the fabric up until the center front crease hangs straight; repin the pants to the elastic (*Diagrams A and B*).

2. Take off the pants.

3. Mark the new waist stitching line and a ⅝" seam above the stitching line on the pant front and back.

4. Alter the pants.

• Fold the pants, right sides together, at the center front; place the front pattern piece on the fabric.

• Match the pattern and the fabric at the original center front line.

• Place a pin at pivot point F; pivot pattern down to the new cutting line marked on the pant side seam.

• Trim the excess fabric at the waist along the pattern cutting line.

• Repeat steps 3 and 4 on the back pattern piece.

5. Use the fabric as a template to make the same adjustment on the front and back pattern pieces (*Diagram C*). Record the changes on the fitting chart for pants (page 139). On future projects, shorten the side curve on the pattern as detailed on page 101.

Note from Nancy: If only one crease bows in, trim only that side of your pants, both front and back.

Pant leg creases bow in.

Diagram A: Smooth fabric up until creases hang straight; repin.

Diagram B: Repin garment to elastic.

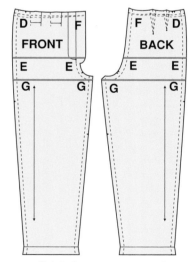

Diagram C: Mark new waist stitching line and ⅝" seam above stitching line.

Hanging Outward

If one hip is higher than the other, by even a slight amount, it may now become noticeable with the crease of one pant leg bowing out.

1. Unpin the pants from the elastic at the side seam until the front crease hangs straight. Repin the pants to the elastic (*Diagram A*).

Note from Nancy: The higher hip has a greater curve, requiring more fabric to go around the shape. This causes the crease to hang outward unless you alter the pattern. Try pinching a 1" tuck at your side seam and watch the pant crease (or the skirt side seam) bow to the side.

2. Take off the pants.

3. Mark the new waist stitching line on the pant front and back. Measure the changes and record them on the fitting chart for pants, page 139.

4. Alter the pants.

• Lay the pants, right side up, on a flat surface.

• Match the front pattern piece to the cut edges of the side that has the high hip.

• Mark the new stitching line on the pattern, adding a ⅝" seam where needed (*Diagram B*). Indicate high hip side on the pattern.

5. Attach the waistband, sewing a smaller seam allowance at the altered pant side.

Pant leg crease bows out.

Diagram A: Unpin pants from elastic until crease hangs straight; repin.

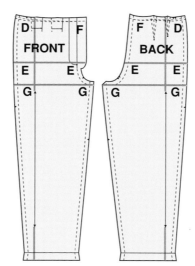

Diagram B: Mark new waist stitching line and ⅝" seam above stitching line.

Reference

Fitting Finesse begins with three important steps: recognizing your figure type, choosing the correct pattern size, and measuring your figure. To make these first steps easy, all the charts you need—including the Personal Fitting Chart and the Personal Fitting Chart for Pants—are collected in this chapter.

If you sew for more than one person, consider photocopying the fitting charts before you use them so that each person can have a chart.

BODY SILHOUETTE CHART

Description	Goal	Best Styles	Best Colors and Fabrics
<u>Pear-shaped:</u> Has greater width at hip than at shoulder	Broaden shoulders and draw eyes away from hip	• Sleeves with pleats or gathers • Shoulder pads • Trims positioned to create vertical lines • Double-breasted jackets • Horizontal lines above waist • Vertical lines below waist for slimming effect—skirts with gores or pants with pleats • Jackets or tunics that end below fullest part of hip	• Textured fabrics and trims above waist to add volume, emphasis to upper body • Crisper fabrics, brighter colors above waist to draw eyes up • One-color outfits, adding emphasis above waist with buttons, trims, accessories (jewelry, scarves, etc.) • Two-tone outfits, with darker color for skirts or pants

Description	Goal	Best Styles	Best Colors and Fabrics
<u>Full-busted:</u> Has upside-down triangular shape, largest at bust	Balance top and bottom of figure to achieve illusion of proportioned silhouette	• Pattern lines to move eyes down, away from bust • Linear emphasis below waist—dropped waists, hip yokes with gathers below waist • Shoulder tucks or pleats to provide softness, add fullness, without emphasizing bust • Blouson tops to flatter figure stylishly, comfortably • Pants or skirts with fullness or weight below waist to create visual balance between top and bottom torso	• Solid-color tops with print or textured skirts • Smooth-textured fabrics without significant shine or luster above waist, textured fabrics below waist • Medium-weight fabrics above waist to conceal body curves • Allover prints with dark backgrounds

Styles for pear-shaped figures

Styles for full-busted figures

BODY SILHOUETTE CHART

Description	Goal	Best Styles	Best Colors and Fabrics
Full-figured: Has wide bust, waist, and hip in proportion to height	Create slimmer look using vertical lines to draw eyes up and down, rather than across body	• Long tunic tops with front plackets • Blouson tops to create soft design lines • Loose fitting jackets or tops in lengths that end below hip • U or V necks to visually draw attention up	• One-color outfits (not necessarily dark color) to coax eye up, make figure seem taller, more slender • Two-color outfits • Soft to medium-weight fabrics to shape around curves without emphasizing body contours • Darker fabrics at heaviest or fullest part of body, lighter colors in slimmest area of body • Dull textures to minimize attention
Description	**Goal**	**Best Styles**	**Best Colors and Fabrics**
Long-waisted: Has added length in upper torso in proportion to bottom of figure	Visually shorten upper torso	• Yokes or wide collars to add width to upper body, visually shorten it • Pockets, epaulets, lapels to draw eye across body • Wide waistbands to shorten upper body	• Any fabrics • Belt colors matched to garments to de-emphasize waistline • Belt colors matched to fabrics below waist to increase length of lower torso • Horizontal stripes, especially above waist, to shorten waist

Styles for full figures

Styles for long-waisted figures

BODY SILHOUETTE CHART

Description	Goal	Best Styles	Best Colors and Fabrics
Short-waisted: Has short upper torso in relation to lower torso	Make upper torso appear longer in proportion to lower half of figure by visually adding length to upper body	• Dropped-waist styles to make body appear longer • Narrow collars, U or V necks to increase upper torso length • Princess styles to draw eye up and down • Vertical lines to visually add length	• All-over prints • Small-print fabrics above waist • Two-piece outfits in one color
Description	**Goal**	**Best Styles**	**Best Colors and Fabrics**
Petite: Has much shorter waist length than average, small bone structure, 5'3" or shorter height	Visually lengthen petite figure to make silhouette appear taller; achieve ⅓ to ⅔ division of figure (upper body to lower body) through use of colors, design features	• V necks, other vertical lines to draw eyes up, add length • Vertical lines plus horizontal lines to add height, fullness • Double-breasted garments to add fullness • Short jackets to keep figure in proportion • Tiered layers to add fullness • Short sleeves to create ⅓ to ⅔ proportions; long jackets with short skirts to create ⅔ to ⅓ reverse proportions	• Small to medium-size prints with white or cream spaces between motifs to add light spaces, fullness • One-color outfits, with shoes and hosiery in neutral tone or matching skirt hemlines to add visual length • Combined design elements (vertical lines, color blocking) to draw eye up for height

Styles for short-waisted figures

Styles for petite figures

BODY SILHOUETTE CHART

Description	Goal	Best Styles	Best Colors and Fabrics
<u>Slim-Tall:</u> Has small bone structure, height of 5'7" or taller, sometimes with longer waist length; may have athletic build, with broad shoulders, and narrow bust, waist, and hip	Maximize the most versatile figure type, by wearing wide variety of patterns, styles	• Yokes, gathers, tucks, ruffles, pocket emphasis • Blouson tops to add curves, dropped waists to soften effect • Layering—combine jackets, vests, blouses, tunics • Dramatic dressing for both day wear and evening wear	• Textured fabrics—bulky woolens, textured tweeds, prints, plaids, nubby fabrics • Accessories used as dramatic accents—large pins, chunky jewelry, big purses, scarves

Styles for slim-tall figures

FRONT WIDTH FITTING CHART

Front width	12"	12½"	13"	13½"	14"	14½"	15"	15½"	16"	16½"	17"	17½"	18"
Misses'/Petite	6	8	10	12	14	16	18	20	22				
Juniors	5	7	9	11	13	15							
Half Size			10½	12½	14½	16½	18½	20½	22½	24½			
Women's							38	40	42	44	46	48	50

Choose your correct blouse, dress, or jacket size by taking your front width measurement (see page 9) and using this chart.

WRINKLE CHART

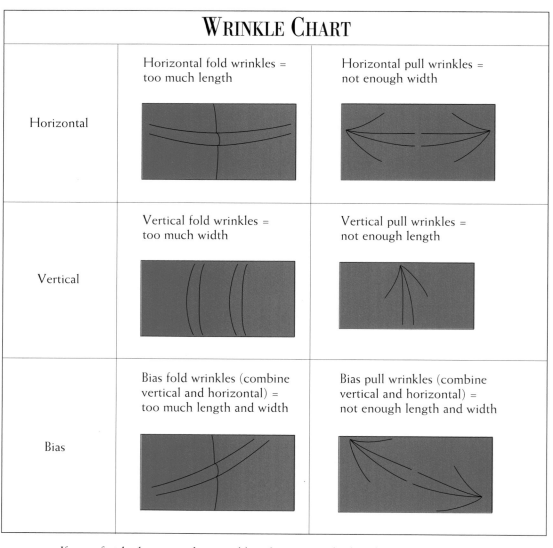

Horizontal

Horizontal fold wrinkles = too much length

Horizontal pull wrinkles = not enough width

Vertical

Vertical fold wrinkles = too much width

Vertical pull wrinkles = not enough length

Bias

Bias fold wrinkles (combine vertical and horizontal) = too much length and width

Bias pull wrinkles (combine vertical and horizontal) = not enough length and width

If your finished garment has wrinkles, determine whether they are caused by too much fabric or too little fabric. Compare them to this chart and then turn to "Fine-tuning the Fit," beginning on page 118, for specific instructions on eliminating each type of wrinkle.

PERSONAL FITTING CHART FOR PANTS

Name:						Date:	
Pattern Type:						Pattern Size:	

	Length	Side Curve	Crotch	Waist	Hip	Thigh	Special Measurements
Pattern Envelope Measurement							
– Your Measurement (include ease)	no ease	no ease	no ease	+1" ease	+3" ease	+2" ease	
= Difference (+/–)							
Alter? (Yes or No)							

To use the pants chart, see page 91 for "Measuring Your Figure" and page 95 for "Measuring the Pattern." Record the measurements and compare them to determine where to make alterations and how much to alter.

In the Special Measurements column, record other information, such as the depth of wrinkles found in the fine-tuning process (see page 122).

If you sew for more than one person, photocopy the chart for each person.

FITTING FINESSE PANT PATTERN SIZE CHART

Hip Measurement	Misses'/Petite	Juniors	Half Size	Women's
34"	6	5		
36"	8	7		
38"	10	9	10½	
40"	12	11	12½	
42"	14	13	14½	
44"	16	15	16½	38
46"	18		18½	40
48"	20		20½	42
50"+	22		22½	44

Choose your correct pant size based on this chart. If your hips are larger than 50", use Misses' size 22, Half Size 22½, or Women's size 44.

PATTERN SIZE CHART

Misses'		XS			S		M		L
	6	8	10	12	14	16	18	20
Bust	30½	31½	32½	34	36	38	40	42
Waist	23	24	25	26½	28	30	32	34
Hip	32½	33½	34½	36	38	40	42	44
Back Waist Length	15½	15¾	16	16¼	16½	16¾	17	17¼

Petite	6	8	10	12	14	16
Bust	30½	31½	32½	34	36	38
Waist	23	24	25	26½	28	30
Hip	32½	33½	34½	36	38	40
Back Waist Length	14½	14¾	15	15¼	15½	15¾

Juniors	5	7	9	11	13	15
Bust	28	29	30½	32	33½	35
Waist	22	23	24	25	26	27
Hip	31	32	33½	35	36½	38
Back Waist Length	13½	14	14½	15	15⅜	15¾

Half Size	10½	12½	14½	16½	18½	20½	22½	24½
Bust	33	35	37	39	41	43	45	47
Waist	27	29	31	33	35	37½	40	42½
Hip	35	37	39	41	43	45½	48	50½
Back Waist Length	15	15¼	15½	15¾	15⅞	16	16⅛	16¼

Women's	38	40	42	44	46	48	50
Bust	42	44	46	48	50	52	54
Waist	35	37	39	41½	44	46½	49
Hip	44	46	48	50	52	54	56
Back Waist Length	17¼	17⅜	17½	17⅝	17¾	17⅞	18